THE LITTLE BOOK OF NEUROSES

ALSO AVAILABLE FROM ALYSON BOOKS
BY MICHAEL THOMAS FORD

Alec Baldwin Doesn't Love Me
& Other Trials From My Queer Life

That's Mr. Faggot to You:
Further Trials From My Queer Life

It's Not Mean If It's True:
More Trials From My Queer Life

THE LITTLE BOOK OF NEUROSES

ONGOING TRIALS FROM MY QUEER LIFE

BY MICHAEL THOMAS FORD

alyson books
los angeles | new york

MANUFACTURED IN THE UNITED STATES OF AMERICA.

THIS TRADE PAPERBACK ORIGINAL IS PUBLISHED BY
ALYSON PUBLICATIONS,
P.O. BOX 4371, LOS ANGELES, CALIFORNIA 90078-4371.
DISTRIBUTION IN THE UNITED KINGDOM BY
TURNAROUND PUBLISHER SERVICES LTD.,
UNIT 3, OLYMPIA TRADING ESTATE, COBURG ROAD, WOOD GREEN,
LONDON N22 6TZ ENGLAND.

FIRST EDITION: NOVEMBER 2001

02 03 04 05 a 10 9 8 7 6 5 4 3 2

ISBN 1-55583-643-7

LIBRARY OF CONGRESS CATALOGING-IN-PUBLICATION DATA
FORD, MICHAEL THOMAS.
   THE LITTLE BOOK OF NEUROSES : ONGOING TRIALS FROM MY
QUEER LIFE / BY MICHAEL THOMAS FORD. — 1ST ED.
   ISBN 1-55583-643-7
   1. HOMOSEXUALITY — HUMOR. 2. GAY MEN — HUMOR. 3. GAY WIT
AND HUMOR. I. TITLE.
PN6231.H57 F677 2001
814'.54 — DC21   2001046074

CREDITS
COVER DESIGN BY MATT SAMS.
COVER PHOTOGRAPHY BY PHILIP PIROLO.

For Dan Cullinane,
who asked me to go to a movie,
and for Patrick Crowe,
who came with him and changed my life.

CONTENTS

About the Title

People always want to know about titles. Where do they come from? Who decides what the best one is for a book? What were you *thinking*?

This is particularly true of my books. My previous three essay collections have had, to say the least, fairly unusual titles. The first one, *Alec Baldwin Doesn't Love Me*, got a lot of attention precisely *because* of the title (porn star Tom Katt's naked chest on the cover didn't hurt either), and the book was noticed by a lot of people who might not have picked it up otherwise. The second collection, *That's Mr. Faggot to You*, also earned its share of readers simply because people wanted to see what a book with that title could possibly be about. Then again, a number of readers complained that they didn't dare read it on the subway or on planes, so it was not universally liked. But the third book, *It's Not Mean If It's True*, seemed to make everyone happy, especially Alec Baldwin (who I think was getting a little tired of being asked just how well he knew me) and bookstore clerks (who don't seem to like saying "Mr. Faggot" all that much).

With the previous books, coming up with titles was fairly painless. That was not the case this time around. I tried several different things, but none of them really worked. In the past, the titles have always come from a title of one of the pieces in the book. But as I assembled the essays I wanted to use, it became apparent that, this time, that approach wasn't going to work. None of them seemed to define the book. It was more like they were working as a team, albeit a dysfunctional one. I came to view them like the contestants on *Survivor,* huddled anxiously under a leaky tarp as they tried to get the rice to cook. No one wanted to be the show-off, probably out of fear of being voted out of the book by the others.

I knew that we would eventually have to call the book *something,* so I occasionally took time to think about the title, usually while I was walking the dog or doing dishes or avoiding my publisher's telephone calls asking me if I'd come up with any good ideas yet. And as I did, I began to think about why I was doing the book at all. (Some of you may be asking this very question. If so, please remember that I thought of it first, and that imitation is not always the sincerest form of flattery.)

Ever since the publication of *Alec Baldwin Doesn't Love Me,* I've gotten a lot of mail. Mostly it's nice mail, notes from people who have read my books or listened to my radio shows and enjoyed them. Every so often someone gets upset about something I've said and decides to tell me off, but even those letters are OK. It's good to know that people are paying attention.

I've noticed over the years a distinct theme running through a lot of this mail, a theme summed up by an E-mail that I received just this morning:

> I've never written a fan letter before, but I just finished your book *It's Not Mean If It's True*—which I bought for a flight from New York to London—and I wanted to drop you a quick note to let you know how much I loved it. It's so nice

to know that there's someone else out there who doesn't get it most of the time. I thought I was the only one who worried about things like my dog sleeping on the bed and my boyfriend not calling enough. I feel much better knowing that you're even more neurotic than I am.

I get letter after letter just like this one, always from readers who really believe that they're somehow out of step with everyone else. Well, I have news: Most of us are completely mentally unwell. It's just that we're not supposed to let on.

I'm not talking about actual mental illness here. I'm talking about the daily neuroses and worries that most of us have but few of us will actually admit to. We live in the Age of Cool, where everyone is supposed to have a handle on their lives and know exactly what they're doing. We have PalmPilots and personal trainers and Saint-John's-wort to keep us together. We know where we want to go and how to get there, and nothing is going to stop us.

This is particularly true for queer people. Gay men are, after all, exceptionally handsome, with perfect bodies, flashing smiles, and haircuts that look like they were just done 20 minutes ago. Lesbians too are chic and hip. Our lives are straight out of an Abercrombie & Fitch catalog, decorated with furnishings from Pottery Barn, and filled with nothing but Martha Stewart dinner parties and nights at the theater. It's like a never-ending episode of *Will & Grace*, with witty friends popping in to tell us how smashing we look in our new Kenneth Cole suits.

Unfortunately, this is all a little too much for some of

us to manage. My own life, for instance, is much less like *Will & Grace* than it is like *Roseanne*. If friends dropped in for an impromptu cocktail party, they would be served Coors and Pop-Tarts. The most recognizable label on my clothing is Levi's. I am not carrying David Crosby's baby. I know that admitting this will probably keep me out of *Out* magazine's Out 100 issue, but it's true. I simply can't keep up. For one thing, I'm too tired. More than that, though, I'm just a big gay mess.

And I'm not alone. There are a lot of people out there like me. This book, I came to see, is for them. Basically, it's a compendium of everything I worry about on a regular basis (as in daily or even hourly). I know, it's hardly uplifting. But it's cheaper than therapy. Besides, I've always liked books written by people who are willing to admit they feel overwhelmed most of the time. When I'm having a particularly awful day, I read books by people like this — writers such as Shirley Jackson, Erma Bombeck, Sandra Tsing Loh, Anne Lamott, or Alison Bechdel. (It's interesting that I've listed no men here. Why is it that guys generally won't own up to feeling this way? Is it like not asking for directions?)

These are people I can relate to, people whose lives are like mine. When Shirley Jackson, in her brilliant essay collection *Life Among the Savages,* admits that even on her best days she couldn't remember all of her children's names and prepare an edible dinner, I'm right there with her. When Sandra Tsing Loh confesses, in *Depth Takes a Holiday,* to spending entire days in bed playing video games instead of writing, I applaud her. And when Anne Lamott — surely the patron saint of the neurotic — writes in

Operating Instructions: A Journal of My Son's First Year that there are times when she wants to throw her infant son out a window because she can't take the crying anymore, I don't feel quite so bad about telling the dog that if he doesn't stop whining, he's going to go to hell and be Hitler's dog.

So, realizing my purpose, the title came easily and everyone—particularly, I imagine, Alec Baldwin—breathed a sigh of relief. I did my part; now it's up to you to do yours. Read and enjoy. And remember, this is a book for my people. Perhaps you are one of us: the many, the tense, the neurotic.

—Michael Thomas Ford

The F Word

I am not a fun person. This may surprise some of you, particularly those of you who find what I write to be, well, funny. And I'm truly sorry to disappoint you. But it's true. I'm not fun.

My friends are frequently asked, particularly by those who have read my books and found them to be amusing, what it's like to be friends with me. (Strangely, people who ask this question generally seem to think that it must be something like spending a drunken evening with Dorothy Parker or perhaps one of the more sarcastic characters from children's literature—say, Eeyore or Paddington after he's just eaten too many sweets.) Usually my friends snort and respond with something like, "It's not a lot of *fun,* I can tell you that."

I think this is a bit unkind of them, particularly when, it could be argued, I usually have the grace not to point out the fact that many of *them* have just the tiniest flaws— mood swings of roller coaster proportions, say, or obsessive-compulsive disorders that cause them to wash their hands 786 times a day—that make knowing them challenging. But I admit they're not far off the mark. I have issues with fun. You might even say, without correction on my part, that I don't know what fun is.

It is true that many funny people are not very much fun to be around in real life. This is because a great many of us are not the most mentally well people you've ever come across. Probably this is genetic or the result of child-hoods spent in forced labor camps. Whatever the cause, most funny people are funny because we're trying to fight something else, something more sinister that lurks in the back of our consciousness, waiting to get us if we let up for even a moment. The humor keeps the monsters at bay, much like the little night-lights many of us insisted on having beside our beds as children.

Most funny people I know are terrified on a daily basis that one day we will no longer find amusement when we look up at the dark cloud we tend to live beneath and that, in an odd way, renews us whenever it opens up and rains on us. It's like we're some kind of freakish reverse Sleeping Beauties: The Good Fairies gave us something special at our christenings—the ability to find humor in lives that might otherwise be too much to look at straight on—and we're afraid that we might use it all up if we aren't careful. Or, as my friend Ed once said, "It's like God gave you just the tiniest little serving of fun, and you're afraid to eat it in case there isn't any more in the refrigerator." This is clearly not a man who grew up fighting with his siblings over the last piece of cheesecake.

At any rate, the fact remains that I am not fun, nor do I particularly recognize fun when it's happening. When someone says to me, "Oh, you should try [fill in the blank with any chosen activity/restaurant/recreational drug]. It's a lot of fun," I am immediately doubtful. *What is fun?* I think to myself. The concept eludes me.

I am not alone in this. My friend Gretchen has a similar problem. A philosophy professor, she spends a great deal of time worrying about things like whether we really exist, and if we do, why. She thinks this is fun. She's wrong, of course, because nothing is actually fun. But that's neither here nor there. The point is that Gretchen, like myself, doesn't understand the concept of fun when it's applied to normal people (i.e., people who aren't philosophy professors or writers). Once, when a potential date asked her what she liked to do for fun, Gretchen replied truthfully and instantly, "I like to think." You can imagine how such a person might be regarded by others. You'd be right.

This would not be such a terrible problem, except Gretchen has two poodles, Blaise and Zoe. Blaise and Zoe, being dogs, like to have fun. Dog fun. This is different, I believe, from people fun, but it is fun nonetheless. The problem is that Gretchen doesn't understand dog fun. She takes Blaise and Zoe to the park and stands there helplessly while they bark at her expectantly.

"They want to have fun," she says grimly, looking at me for help.

Now, dog fun I understand. It is a simple, defined thing chiefly characterized by lots of running about aimlessly. So I pick up a ball or a stick and I throw it. Blaise and Zoe chase madly after it, tails wagging. This goes on for some time, until they or I tire of it.

"Was that fun?" Gretchen asks timidly.

"Not for me," I tell her. "But the dogs are happy."

People fun is an entirely different thing. Most people I know are quite adept at having fun. Yet none of them can really explain to me *why* certain things are fun. "I love going out dancing," my friend Sophia said the other night. "It's so much fun."

"Why?" I asked her, completely unable to imagine that going out, let alone dancing, could in any way resemble fun.

"I don't know," she said. "I just feel good when I do it. It's *fun*, you know?"

No, I don't know. I do not like to go out. I do not like to dance. And this disturbs my friends, all of whom are desperate for me to have fun. Sometimes, they tell me, I *almost* have fun. But I never quite get there. "It's like there's this switch in your head," my friend Dan said the other day. "You'll be almost having fun, and suddenly it goes off. You can actually see it in your face. It's weird."

I suppose it is. Dan thinks it's my Baptist upbringing. He says that there's this gigantic reservoir of guilt in my brain, and whenever I start to have fun the dam opens and I'm drenched with an overwhelming sense of doing something wrong. Perhaps. But I honestly think it's just that I don't get it.

I feel the need to explain now that it's not like I don't *enjoy* things. I like going to baseball and hockey games. I like going camping. I like napping. Yet whenever I do these things with people (except the napping, which is generally a solitary undertaking) I inevitably get hit with, "Why aren't you having fun?"

"Why do you think I'm not having fun?" I ask wearily, because until that moment I was enjoying myself.

"You just don't seem to be having fun," is the standard answer.

At this point I sometimes feel the need to do something demonstrative, something to prove without question that I really am having a good time. "More defense!" I

4

might bellow at the fellows on the ice, or perhaps, "Wow, those rapids were *fast*." If pushed, I might even resort to doing a little dance with a team mascot or waving my hands in the air and screaming.

"Now you're being hostile," is generally the response I get from whomever I'm with.

"Was I a fun child?" I asked my sister recently. She's 10 years older and therefore had the opportunity to observe my behavior fairly closely.

"Not really," she said. "You always looked like you were waiting for bad news."

Maybe that's it. Maybe I'm convinced that if I actually experience fun, it will all be downhill from there. It's like when you spend all those years thinking about what your first time having sex will be like, and then it happens and all you can think is, *Is that* it?

Also, I am a writer. Writers, in general, *observe* things. But we don't necessarily experience them in the way that normal people do. Several weeks ago I was taken, against my will, to an amusement park by my boyfriend. Patrick is a fun person. He understands fun. He likes it. He's good at it. This is one of the things I love about him. It's like living with someone who can dance beautifully: I watch him doing it and I'm filled with a wonder that it comes so effortlessly to him when my own attempts at it resemble a profoundly retarded child attempting to sing opera.

Now, for the fun-deficient, amusement parks are just below eye surgery on the pleasure scale. But I went, because I knew Patrick would enjoy it and because I knew I would enjoy being with him, even if I wasn't too thrilled about the idea of things like rides and crowds and the potential for vomiting. And not five seconds after we entered the park I found myself strapped into a chair that was attached to a tower. A very tall tower. I looked over at Patrick, who was strapped into the chair next to me, and asked innocently, "What does this do?"

Before he could answer I found myself being hurled into the air at a very high rate of speed. I looked up and saw that we were, as far as I could tell, being launched into the sun. And then, just as suddenly, we stopped going up, hung in the air for a second, and plunged back to earth. We bounced a few times, gently, and then I was released from my chair.

As we walked away from the ride Patrick turned to me and said, with some concern, "I watched your face as we went up. Your expression didn't change, not even once. You may as well have been sitting on the couch in front of the television."

This doesn't surprise me. Because I wasn't really experiencing the ride as a ride. I do recall, as we lifted off, thinking, *So this is what it feels like to be shot into the sky.* But it didn't really occur to me that it was happening to *me* and that I was supposed to *react* to it by screaming (like everyone else did) or wetting my pants (as one little boy did). I was simply observing it, storing the memory for future use; for example, if one of the characters in one of my novels is ever involved in a training mission for a voyage to Venus.

I tried explaining this to Patrick, but I don't think I did a very good job. For the rest of the day, as we went on one ride after another, I often caught him sneaking glances at me. I know he was wondering what kind of man he'd taken up with and perhaps was even thinking of ways to gently break it to me that he might prefer to be with someone who had, say, a soul. Several times he took my hand and said soothingly, "You poor thing," as if I was clearly having the worst time since Joan of Arc was invited to her own barbecue.

I *wasn't* having a bad time, but I knew there was little use in trying to convince him of this. People who are good at fun don't really understand those of us who aren't. And for some reason, amusement parks are always a battleground for those of us on opposite sides of the fun issue. "I *despise* amusement parks," my friend Robrt said when I talked to him later in the week. "Every time Todd and I go to one and I refuse to go on the rides he says, 'Honey, it's OK if you're afraid. You can admit it.' I'm not afraid. I just think rides are stupid. But he thinks I'm lying, and then I feel I have to prove to him that I'm not afraid, so I go on them and want to push him off just when we reach the highest point of whatever idiotic thing we're on."

Perhaps I'm being too cynical. Maybe all I need to do is give it a try. But I'm not even sure how to go about it. Maybe going out dancing *would* be…interesting. But I can't imagine why. Early on in our relationship, Patrick casually remarked as we were walking by a bar near my house, "That place is really fun to hang out in."

When I didn't respond, he said, "What's wrong?"

"Nothing," I told him. The fact was, I was trying to figure out how to explain to him that he was dating someone for whom fun was not an option. Because, frankly, just the idea of being in a gay bar at all is absolutely horrifying to me. The idea of it being *fun* is something I am not even willing to consider, even on my most upbeat days.

The older I get, the more I resent the pressure to have fun. "What do you do for fun out there in California?" my mother asks when she calls, making me grind my teeth. "Drink heavily and wait to die," I feel like saying. "What can we do this weekend that would be fun?" my friends ask, and immediately I feel pressured to come up with something, and fast.

Recently Patrick announced that we will be taking a trip to Las Vegas in the near future. "It will be fun," he said decidedly.

"Will it?" I asked neutrally.

He narrowed his eyes. I knew he was thinking about the amusement park incident. "You're going to have fun on this trip if it kills you."

"Just remember," I told him. "You can't remarry for two years, and you have to wear black."

According to my dictionary, the word *fun* is derived from the Middle English word *fonnen,* which means "to dupe." This, it seems to me, is exactly the problem. We're told that we *have* to have fun; otherwise we must be depressed or angry or dead. Not content to just let us sit quietly enjoying the moment, the Fun Cheerleaders come by to ruin everything, waving their pom-poms in our faces and attempting to get us to stand up and do the wave with them. Well, I've had enough of it. I say down with fun and those who promote it shamelessly. Let's hear it for plain old contentedness or even mild satisfaction. Are they so bad?

The next time someone asks me if I'm having fun, I think I'll smile pleasantly and say, "Yes, I'm contemplating setting you on fire." Now, *that* would be fun.

Relationship Tips for the Neurotically Inclined

Once upon a time, being neurotic was fun. Those of us with, shall we say, more finely tuned personalities were treated with utmost care, not to mention great psychiatric interest. To aid us in our endeavors we were presented with such intriguing items as fainting couches, smelling salts, and fans. The more ambitious of us could look forward to spending copious amounts of time in bed, being sent to spas for weeks on end, and perhaps being bled by leeches. It was a glorious time, marked chiefly by pallor, fidgetiness, and lots of sighing.

Things are not so good now. We as a culture have become far less tolerant of peevishness and fretting, and over the years neurosis as a defining personality trait has seen a sharp decline in popularity, to the point where it now it hovers somewhere between obsessive hand washing and bed-wetting. This raises problems for those among us who stubbornly cling to our neuroses, refusing to let go like thumb suckers hanging on to our favorite blankets for dear life.

But fear not. There is hope for a resurrection. A number of years ago someone published the enormously popular book *How to Live With a Neurotic Cat*. This was followed, inevitably, by the similarly themed *How to Live With a Neurotic Dog*. These were funny books, giving cat and dog owners much to chuckle about. But their chief value seems to have been overlooked, which is that they were wonderful training manuals for those who knew how to use them. They were, in short, filled with tips on how to be neurotic.

Now, constant furniture shredding and tail chewing are all well and good if you have four feet and answer to a single name. (No, Cher does not count, as she has only two feet.) But for those of us with brains larger than your average lemon, it takes slightly more than that. With that in mind, I offer here an easy-to-follow plan designed to take full advantage of the neurotic's natural abilities. This particular set of instructions and practical exercises is focused on relationships, as that seems to be the area where the neurotic excels and also where the most challenges are faced.

TIP 1: ASSUME THE WORST

Relationships, for the neurotic, are the perfect breeding ground for worry. When approached correctly, they can provide endless opportunities for exercising the natural inclination to believe that in any given situation the most unpleasant outcome is inevitable. This can begin on the very first date, where you can immediately begin thinking of reasons for there not being a second date. Should the relationship miraculously continue, each day that it goes forward is another occasion for gut-wrenching anxiety. Particularly excellent moments for perfecting this approach include promised phone calls that don't come, nights when your beloved is "out with friends," and the first time your partner answers "Me too" in response to your "I love you."

EXERCISE: Make a list of every possible reason your relationship could fail. Do not forget to take into account differences in sleeping habits, food preferences, height, allergies, religious practices, age, blood type, income, toothpaste squeezing technique, television viewing habits, sexual turn-ons, musical tastes, and the absolutely-sure-to-be-devastating Yankees versus Mets schism.

TIP 2: KEEP IT ALL INSIDE

This can be a particularly difficult thing to master, but if you can do it, it will serve you well. In general, it is more satisfying for the neurotic to voice any and all concerns or worries that come up, as it puts one's partner in the position of having to be reassuring. There are, however, occasions when it is far more pleasurable to keep your thoughts to yourself. Why? Because you're probably wrong in whatever it is you're worried about, and letting your partner know what you're thinking will deprive you of the delicious joy that comes from having something painful to gnaw on. This technique is most successful at times when simply asking a question would clear everything up—for example, after finding an empty condom wrapper under your boyfriend's bed (he probably hasn't cleaned under there since long before he met you) and running into someone on the street whom your partner greets cordially but fails to introduce you to (surely a former trick).

EXERCISE: Think about an offhand remark your boyfriend made that for some reason made you suspicious, such as the time you were out together and, indicating a man in the bar where you were getting a drink, he said, "That guy has done *everyone* in town." Wonder—but don't ask—if this includes your boyfriend. Imagine what they might have done together. Become irrationally angry at him for saying something that he should have known would make you unhappy. Again, do not say anything. It is much more satisfying to seethe.

TIP 3: CONSTANTLY COMPARE YOURSELF TO HIS EXES

Exes are prime fodder for making yourself neurotic. After all, they've gone before you, so of course your boyfriend *must* be comparing you to them, right? It's only fair, then, that you do the same thing. This is particularly easy for gay men because we always seem to remain in contact with our exes (proof, I think, that we're all neurotic to start with). If your boyfriend keeps pictures of his exes, all the better. Visuals add depth and clarity to the worry. But even if there are no physical reminders, you always have mental ones. Be sure to note every time your boyfriend mentions an ex and in what context. Examine his face closely (but covertly) to see if he smiles when thinking about the men in his past. Provide opportunities for him to comment on his exes, then go over and over his responses in your mind—preferably late at night, while lying next to your boyfriend and resenting him for being able to sleep while you fret. The more bold neurotic may

even go so far as to be agonizingly direct, employing questions such as, "Did [insert name of ex] do that for you in
bed?" "Did you love him as much as you love me?" and "Is
my dick bigger than his?"

EXERCISE: If possible, make a list of all of your
boyfriend's exes. Include one-night stands. Go through
the list one by one, thoroughly outlining the reasons each
of them annoys you. Wonder what your boyfriend did in
bed with them. Wonder if he took them to the same places
he takes you. Wonder if he called them the same silly
names or laughed the same way when *they* tickled him.
Deeply resent every moment he spent with them. Most
important, be sure to completely ignore the fact that *you*
have just as many (if not more) men in your past and that
those experiences have absolutely no effect on how much
you love your current guy. This would be far too emotionally healthy and could threaten to undo all the hard work
you've done.

TIP 4: LOOK FOR CLUES

Think of this as a scavenger hunt. Or perhaps a police
investigation. You're looking for clues—any piece of physical evidence that will enable you to worry about what your
boyfriend is up to and what he's hiding from you.
Particularly good finds include scraps of paper with phone
numbers, photographs showing your boyfriend with his
arm around men unfamiliar to you, E-mails from people
with suggestive screen names, pornographic magazines or
videos, ticket stubs left in coat pockets, cards that accom-

panied flower deliveries and are signed only with initials, and phone numbers programmed into his phone. Be sure to check medicine cabinets, car glove compartments, shoeboxes in closets, and his wallet (make sure he's in the shower or asleep). More advanced techniques include secretly marking the lube bottle to see if any is used in between your visits, scrolling through the call log on his cell phone, and counting the number of condoms left in the box.

EXERCISE: Keep an evidence log. In it write down everything you find that seems suspicious. NOTE: It is important never to take the actual items. After all, you don't want your boyfriend to *know*, do you? That would take all the fun out of it. (See Tip 2). Instead, repeatedly go over the "proof" you've collected, creating elaborate scenarios around each tiny morsel. That ticket stub from a ball game, for example: Who did he go with? What did they do afterward? That phone number: Is it a friend's? Why does it just say "Carl" on it? Should you call it and hang up? And is that bar smell on the paper? Ah, the thrill of it all.

TIP 5: CREATE A SUPPORT GROUP

Being neurotic alone is satisfying; doing it with others is nirvana. Having someone to bounce your suspicions, worries, and general fears off of gives you the opportunity to bring your neuroses to life, and if you choose wisely, you can have an unending source of inspiration. This is particularly true if the other person (or persons) in your support group is just as neurotic as you are. A good support person will know when to reassure you and when to egg you on. For instance, you know you've found yourself a perfect accomplice if, when you suggest that you think your boyfriend might be losing interest, your friend responds not with "Don't be ridiculous" but with "Well, he *has* been spending a lot of time without you." Good choices for support staff include your own exes (who knows you better?), fag hags (no matter what they say, they want you for themselves), and your mother (ditto on both previous examples). When employing this technique, be sure to schedule regular meeting times—nightly phone calls or Wednesday dinners out are good—so as to have something to look forward to.

EXERCISE: Begin interviewing possible candidates for your support group position(s). Make a list of the most neurotic people you know. Invite each one to lunch or out for drinks. During conversation, throw out a starter question. For example, "Do you find that you have less sex the longer you're with someone?" Gauge the response and mark the performance on a scale of 1 to 10, depending on how much more neurotic you feel about your own relationship based on their answers. Narrow your list of contestants to five finalists. Have brunch with all of them at once. Halfway through, turn the conversation to relationships again. Take notes (clandestinely) and rank the five in order of their ability to raise doubts and worries in your mind. This is your team. Number 1 is the captain; the other four are your backup squad.

SELLING OUT

OK, I've been watching *Who Wants to Be a Millionaire*. But not to see if I can guess all the answers. The questions are those random kind that you just either know or don't know. No, the best part, for me, is seeing people get totally confused about the simplest things on national television. By the time the contestants get to the highest levels, they're so unnerved that they'll convince themselves of anything. Except the gay players. They all seem to do pretty well. When a poor straight guy got confused the other night on a question about which of the following is not a type of mushroom and thought a morel was a kind of eel, I snickered, knowing that any self-respecting queen would have answered correctly in two seconds flat and ended up with $64,000. The same with the fellow who didn't know how many children Captain Von Trapp had in *The Sound of Music*. He passed on the question rather than risk losing a little money, and you could just hear queens all across America shouting, "Do. Re. Mi. Fa. So. La. Ti. you hetero idiot!" as they counted the seven children off on their fingers.

Anyway, it seems that everyone is obsessed with this show, and that's no big surprise. Americans are fascinated by money and by other people trying to win money. And who doesn't want to be a millionaire? Although really the show should be called *Who Wants to Be a Half-Millionaire*, since the taxes on those prizes are 49%. But you get the idea. Those of us who don't have a half million want to see other people get it, or at least try to get it while we sit at home saying, "I would have gotten that one."

While ratings for *Who Wants to Be a Millionaire* have been stellar, the show's popularity seems to be dipping a bit now that several other more interesting shows like *The Weakest Link* and *Survivor* have appeared. I think, though, that with a little bit of tweaking they could get the show back on top. The trick is to simply play to other great American obsessions.

Imagine, for example, *Who Wants to Weigh 500 Pounds.* Next to money, weight is the great American obsession. Many of us are trying to lose a few pounds, and thin is most definitely in. But what would happen if we offered people money to *gain* weight? In this variation of the game show, thin, beautiful people would be given the chance to make big money by getting fat. For every pound gained they would be given a cash prize, with the amount increasing at various levels.

The first few pounds probably wouldn't be a big deal. Most people would be willing to pack on 10 or 20 pounds if they were given, say, $5,000 or $10,000. But what would happen when the bar was raised to 50 or 100 pounds? How many of us would gain that much weight for cash, especially if we were really weight-conscious to begin with? It would be a fascinating struggle between beauty and wealth. If you had, for example, a bunch of supermodels or aerobics instructors, watching them decide between thinness and early retirement would provide weeks of fun. Every episode would involve weighing the contestants and asking if they want to progress to the next level of obesity. The host could wave platters of Hostess products before their anxious faces, tempting them to ever-greater levels of hugeness just for the sake of taking home that elusive half a million. It would be human drama at its most theatrical.

Or what about *Who Wants to Be a Homosexual?* This would be even better. Heterosexual contestants — preferably men — would be presented with a series of choices, each one leading them closer and closer to a queer life. The first step might be agreeing to spend a night out dancing in a gay bar, say for $2,500. From there they would be challenged to march in a pride parade wearing only leather shorts, walk down a main street of some medium-sized Midwestern city holding hands with someone of the same gender, come out to a family member, and attend a Liza Minnelli concert. As the weeks went on, they would have to decide if a same-sex kiss was worth the cash payout, whether being the passive partner in oral sex for $16,000 was preferable to being the active partner for $25,000, and, in the final week, if the indignity of being anally penetrated on national television could be paid for with that much desired half a million.

Just like on *Who Wants to Be a Millionaire*, contestants would be allowed to stop at any point and walk away with the cash they'd accumulated. If they agreed to go on and did not perform the assigned task successfully, their money would be taken away and they would be left with nothing. And should a contestant reach the final level and pass the anal sex test, he would be rewarded with not only the money but a Hugo Boss wardrobe, an entire collection of Erasure albums, the keys to a condo in South Beach, and a lifetime subscription to both *Out* and *Genre.*

This would be even better than the fat thing. Imagine watching people decide how much being perceived as gay was worth. Would they stop at $32,000, or would they only be willing to be gay for $120,000? How much would it take to buy off male fears about sucking dick and taking it up the butt? I'd love to find out.

Of course, we already have some idea of the answer. Porn actors regularly get paid for assuming different positions in their films. Much of the gay world watched, literally, as former porn icon Ryan Idol went from being a straight guy who would only allow other actors to blow him to a skilled cocksucker himself. With each film, Idol did a little more, as long as he was paid more. And he isn't alone. Hollywood is filled with actors who will play gay as long as the paycheck is right. Remember Will Smith? When he had to kiss Anthony Michael Hall in *Six Degrees of Separation* a few years back, he made sure to talk about how awful the smooch was in every interview he did.

We won't even get into all the Tinseltown figures who have donned drag or feigned queerness in the past couple of years just because the money was right. Or those who have kept their real queerness secret for exactly the same reason. How many people are there who are willing to trade who they are for the security of a paycheck and continued status? How many of us choose to do it in both small and large ways on a daily basis? Like the contestants in these proposed game shows, do we continually weigh what our identities are worth, selling ourselves for another week of living large? Yes, money can make people do a lot of things they would never do for free. But you have to wonder: at what cost?

STRAIGHT NO MORE

A Paper Presented at the Seventh Annual Sex and Sexuality Symposium, Being the Results of a Study Performed by Percy S. Hollister, MD

As many of you know, a recent study by one of our esteemed colleagues purported to prove that persons who once defined themselves as actively homosexual could, through a combination of therapy and reparative treatment, reverse their sexual orientation and embark upon what one researcher described as "healthy, normal lives as functioning heterosexuals." Like many of you, I found this claim to be most interesting. However, in reviewing the results of this groundbreaking study, it occurred to me that while much has been done in the way of examining the possibilities for homosexual-to-heterosexual transformation, to date there have been no studies investigating the possibilities of the reverse.[1]

To that end, I undertook a yearlong study to determine if, in fact, persons suffering from the problem of unwanted heterosexuality could successfully transition to a homosexual lifestyle. Here are the results.

PARTICIPANTS

Wanting to maintain gender parity as much as possible, I endeavored to recruit equal numbers of men and women for my study. Finding participants proved easier than expected, particularly after I hit upon the idea of placing advertisements in the back of magazines such as *The New Yorker, Martha Stewart Living, Playgirl, Soldier of Fortune,* and the "LPGA Newsletter."

All applicants were asked to submit a detailed sexual history, along with a questionnaire designed to gauge their level of homosexual interest. This allowed me to weed out the merely prurient, those who mistakenly thought the experiment to be some kind of lottery, and those who had meant to send in the coupon for the *Church Potluck Recipes of Cobb County* cookbook that seemed to mysteriously be advertised in every periodical in which our ad appeared.

In the end, I compiled a pool of 250 participants, made up equally of females and males. The ages of the participants ranged from 18 years to 72 years, with the average age being 34. Of those chosen for the study, 64% were unmarried, 27% were married, and 9% were divorced.

METHODOLOGY

While the gay-to-straight "reparative therapy" experiment that I was attempting to re-create relied solely on recorded interviews and the subjects' own claims, it was my wish to undertake a far more exhaustive and controlled experiment. To achieve this, all 250 participants were flown to New York[2] and set up in a block of prewar brownstones on the upper west side. Each was given his (here I use the grammatically correct but frustrating male pronoun with no offense to the women among us) own apartment, tastefully decorated with furnishings commonly known to be popular with homosexuals.[3]

Hidden cameras installed in each room of each apartment provided my team of assistants with round-the-clock coverage of each participant. In addition, each person was required to attend daily check-ins with a counselor as well as group meetings with his peers. In this way, a thorough accounting of each participant's behavior was collected, thus eliminating the possibility of clouding the results with erroneous claims in either direction.

THE COURSE OF TREATMENT

The project lasted for a period of three months and utilized a combination of traditional therapy and a five-step participatory activity program. During the initial counseling sessions, participants were asked to state why they thought that they were engaging in heterosexual behavior. Based on the most common response—"Because everyone else was doing it"—it became apparent that for many of the subjects, heterosexuality was simply the result of peer pressure. Less common, but no less fascinating, answers to the question included "Because I don't know how to dress well"; "Because my mother told me to be"; and "Because I don't want God to turn me into a pillar of salt."

Further sessions with participants, in which we discussed their childhoods and early sexual experiences, gave rise to even more intriguing revelations, and I can say with what I think is incontrovertible, proof-backed authority that for the first time we have been able to trace the onset of what I am terming Temporary Heterosexual Deviation to three primary sources: extensive viewing of *The Waltons* at an early age, excessive exposure to polyester garments, and being forced to participate in team sports.

Having pinpointed the causes of THD, it was then time to begin reversing the unfortunate effects of the disorder. This, as you might imagine, was not easy. While all of the participants expressed a strong desire to become homosexual, it took considerable work for them to overcome ingrained sociosexual responses and break the patterns of heterosexual behavior.

Step 1 began the process gently by having participants stand in front of mirrors and repeat the phrase, "I *can* be gay," for several minutes. Each person was asked to imagine himself living a happy homosexual life, free of the restrictions imposed by the heterosexual lie. When this was achieved, we progressed to the next step.

Step 2 was a ceremony designed to help the participants leave behind their old heterosexual lives and begin their new homosexual lives. With the help of a group of Radical Faeries, a fire pit was built in Central Park. While gathering around the ceremonial flames, each person was asked to throw into the fire those things that reminded him of his old heterosexual self while simultaneously publicly declaring his commitment to homosexuality. A meticulous record of the items surrendered to the flames was kept, with some of the more telling objects being numerous copies of *The Joy of Sex*, the keys to station wagons, videos of Tom Hanks films[4], diaphragms, Erica Jong novels, and boxer shorts with pictures on them. Following the ceremony the subjects held hands and sang a medley of show tunes, culminating in a weepy rendition of "Over the Rainbow."

Step 3 found our subjects claiming their new homosexual identities. This was done in several ways. Some participants elected to choose new names for themselves that fit their new personalities. For the men, the most common choices were Stephen, Robert, Jon, Tyler, and Christian. Names favored by women included Jean, Cris, Wendy, Patty, and Andie. Sam was chosen by two members of each group.

Having selected their new names, the subjects were then sent on shopping excursions. Given new credit cards with $500 limits[5], they were each asked to outfit themselves for their new gay lives. No other guidelines were given, as the goal was to see to what extent the natural homosexual tendencies latent in each participant would emerge.

Again, the results are telling. Fully three quarters of the male subjects returned in the afternoon carrying bags from Abercrombie & Fitch, with the remaining quarter having elected to patronize Banana Republic, J. Crew, Barneys, and Macy's. The women, on the other hand, overwhelmingly headed for the L.L. Bean outlet and Eastern Mountain Sports.

Having now put on the trappings of homosexuality, we proceeded to **Step 4,** which came to be known as "First Date." In this stage of treatment, which took place approximately 10 weeks into the experiment, the subjects were paired up for practice dates. Once partnered—a state achieved through random draw to eliminate the stress of personal choice—the couples were sent out into New York for an evening of homosexual fun. We arranged for the male couples to attend a performance of *The Lion King,* while female couples were sent to a WNBA game.

All in all, the dates were a success. Most participants reported that, for the first time, they felt like they were living the lives they were meant to live. For many, it was a defining moment, perhaps best summed up in the words of one ecstatic female participant who said, "Now I know how my stupid boyfriend could sit there watching football for four hours straight. Those chicks are *hot!*" Truer words, I think, were never spoken.

We now come to the final and probably most controversial step in the study. **Step 5,** or what I call "The Big Test," was designed to determine just how well our treatment had taken with participants. In effect, I wanted to see whether the transition to homosexuality was one that could be maintained over the long haul. To ascertain this, we presented each participant with a test designed to challenge the sexual response. These challenges ranged from leaving heterosexually oriented pornography in rooms to having actual undercover operatives attempt to seduce the subjects. While I realize this is hardly orthodox, it provided us with valuable information regarding the "slip" factor in conversion therapy.

I am happy to report that an astonishingly small percentage of participants—only 2%—succumbed to our test. And of these five individuals, four were later discovered to have been plants working for the religious right. The remaining failure claimed to have been thinking of women the whole time she was engaging in heterosexual sex with an undercover operative. And as she was taking the active role in anal penetration, we elected to declare the incident statistically insignificant.

CONCLUSION

Having heard the results of my experiment, I think you will agree that the conclusions that can be drawn from this material are most exciting. It is my firm conviction that a permanent transition from heterosexuality to homosexuality can be made by any person determined enough to take the step. No longer will those tortured by heterosexuality and the guilt that frequently accompanies it have to suffer. No longer do those with unfulfilling sex lives have to live without joy. We can change them. We can make them better than they were. There is hope for those suffering from THD. And where there is hope, there is also a better wardrobe.

ENDNOTES

1. This does not, of course, include the now-famous experiment conducted by Dr. James Ryalls in which it was shown that heterosexual men, if given vast quantities of beer and shown porn films, could fairly easily be convinced to engage in homosexual behavior. The results of those experiments were, with very few exceptions, temporary and the participants' accounts unreliable since, as most stated, "I don't remember anything. I must have passed out."
2. Special thanks to Virgin Airlines.
3. Special thanks to Pottery Barn.
4. Particularly those also featuring Meg Ryan.
5. Special thanks to Visa.

So You Want to Be a Porn Star

OK, you've seen the movies and thought, *These guys get paid for doing that?* You've got a big dick or a great body or a handsome face. Maybe you even have all three. But is that really enough to make it in the high pressure world of porn stardom? Take this scientifically designed quiz to see what your potential Porn Star Rating is.

1. Your idea of foreplay is:
   (a) A walk along the beach talking about your dreams
   (b) A full body massage
   (c) Tugging your jock down

2. If someone tells you to "fluff up," you:
   (a) Put the towels in the dryer
   (b) Find the nearest available mouth and use it
   (c) Go in search of a blow dryer and some gel

3. When accepting a delivery from your UPS man, you:
   (a) Ask him if he has any other packages that need special handling
   (b) Ask him where to sign
   (c) Ask him how his day is going

4. Fill in the blank: "I'm going to _____ you until you can't take any more."
   (a) Nag

(b) Audit

(c) Fuck

5. As a kid, your favorite game to play with your G.I. Joe was:
   (a) Marine Barracks Gang Bang
   (b) Rescue the POWs
   (c) Tea Party With Barbie and Skipper

6. You would douche for the following occasion:
   (a) A rectal exam
   (b) Going to the grocery store with the humpy produce manager
   (c) Prostate surgery

7. In your opinion, the best movie ever made is:
   (a) *Casablanca*
   (b) *Butt Bruisers III: Deep Impact*
   (c) *All About Eve*

8. The thought of hot lights and a camera crew around your bed makes you:
   (a) Nervous
   (b) Suspicious
   (c) Hard as a rock

9. If you stumbled upon two guys going at it in the sauna at the gym, you would:
   (a) Tell them to make room for you
   (b) Tell the management to throw them out
   (c) Tell your friends how rude it was

10. You can imagine yourself being called which of the
following:
(a) Mr. President
(b) Miss Thing
(c) Jack Hammer

ANSWERS:

1. (c)
2. (b)
3. (a)
4. (c)
5. (a)
6. (b)
7. (b)
8. (c)
9. (a)
10. (c)

SCORING:

Give yourself five points for each correct answer.

0–10: Stick with the relationship quizzes in *Cosmo.* Porn
stardom is way beyond you.

15–20: You'd better rent a few more porn videos and see
what they're all about. When you get the whole
top/bottom thing figured out, try again.

25–30: Sorry, you're just a slut. It isn't the same thing. But
if we film an orgy scene, we'll call you. Really.

35–40: Not bad at all. We'd be happy to set up a screen test. Just remember, when the casting director is happy, you get the job.

45–50: Chi Chi LaRue is waiting with open, um, arms for your arrival. Lube yourself up and get ready for your close-up.

HEART FAILURE

With Valentine's Day coming up, my thoughts turn, naturally, to romance. More specifically, I can't help thinking how bad gay men are at it. I know I've complained about this before, but this time of year I'm reminded of it even more usual because, odd as it seems, most of the guys I know face February 14 with a sense of doom.

There are a number of reasons for this, but I think we can trace the origins back to one specific moment in every queer boy's life: Valentine's Day in the third grade.

You remember this day. Most likely a week or so before, the teacher had you decorate a box of some kind with hearts and flowers and cupids. This was your very own valentine card box. Trimmed with lace and sparkling with glitter, it was perfect for all of the valentines your classmates were going to stuff inside it.

As for the valentines themselves, you were supposed to have made or bought one for each person in the class. Maybe your mom went out and bought a package of cards with the Peanuts gang on them, or perhaps Garfield or Bugs Bunny or some other popular character. Maybe you made your own from red construction paper. Then, armed with a list of your fellow students' names, you were expected to make sure everyone had a card from you, preferably all of the same size and type.

But this was never how it worked. There were always people in the class who you liked more than others. For these people, you saved the best cards, the ones with the cutest pictures and wittiest inscriptions. Everyone else could have the Peppermint Patty and Lucy cards, but there were those for whom the Woodstocks and Snoopys were reserved.

Inevitably, one of these people was the object of a first crush, usually some boy whom, for whatever reason, you wanted to have as your special friend. Maybe you dreamed about him or had fantasies of holding his hand on the swings. Probably you didn't have any real understanding of what attracted you to him. You just knew that thinking about him made you feel funny. But you saved the best valentine for him, making sure your printing was neat and your message meaningful. No generic "Happy Valentine's Day" for his card. Oh, no. Something along the lines of "Knowing you makes every day special" was better, or, if you were feeling particularly daring, the suggestive "Be mine."

On the big day, after far too many sugar cookies had been eaten and cups of red Kool-Aid drunk, it was time to go around the room stuffing your valentines into one another's boxes. This ritual was accompanied by much giggling and nervousness. It was, after all, your first taste of romance, however innocent. You tried to avoid looking at your own box while you went about your business, but as soon as you were finished delivering your cards it was a mad dash back to your seat to see what was waiting for you.

Cards from friends were nice, but they weren't what you were after. You wanted to find that one card that would make the day really special. Tearing open envelopes with a vengeance, you quickly noted the sender's name and went on to the next. Then, if you were lucky, you'd come to the one you were waiting for, a card from the object of your affection. Holding your breath, you opened it to see what it was.

And then you were crushed. There was no special card with a secret message. No "Be mine" or "My heart belongs to you." Probably it was a generic Mickey Mouse card or maybe one with racing cars on it. Inside was a hastily scribbled signature and nothing more. Looking around, you saw that everyone else had received exactly the same card.

Even worse, the boy you liked didn't seem to even notice all the work you put into his card. It was jumbled in a pile with all the rest as he went in search of another cookie. Or, the most crushing blow of all, you saw it lying on the floor where he had carelessly dropped it, some-one's dusty footprint spoiling the message you'd so care-fully written.

For most of us, this was the last time we let ourselves have romantic thoughts. Seeing our hearts—both figura-tive and literal—trampled by the uncaring feet of a reject-ing suitor, we gave up. The disappointment was simply too much. And now when Valentine's Day comes along we play it safe, waiting to see what the other guy is going to do first before we start making our own plans.

A couple of weeks ago, I asked my boyfriend what he wanted to do for Valentine's Day. "I don't know," he said warily. "What do *you* want to do?"

I understand his caution. This will be our first Valentine's Day together. In some ways, it's a test of the relationship. If one of us does something more extravagant than the other, it could be a disaster. I have a friend who went to Valentine's Day dinner with his boyfriend armed with what he thought was the perfect gift—tickets to a show they both wanted to see. But before he could present them to his lover, he found himself being handed a small box. Inside was a wedding band. Dessert was a bitter affair.

I'm not sure what I'm going to get my boyfriend. But I do know that I'm saving the Snoopy valentine for him. This time, I don't think he'll step on it.

BUYER'S REMORSE

It is now possible to buy back your childhood.

A couple of months ago, I made my first visit to eBay, the online auction site that has taken the world by storm. I'd heard about eBay from several friends who had been using it for some time, but I'd never seen it for myself. Frankly, I didn't see what the big deal was. From what I'd heard, it seemed like a lot of people selling the crap from their garages and attics. I spend most of my time trying to get rid of crap I already have. I couldn't imagine buying more of it.

But then I logged on, and everything changed.

You know how every so often you'll suddenly remember a happy moment from your childhood when you were playing with a particular toy or game, and you wish you could capture that moment again because you were happier then than ever since? Well, now you can, thanks to eBay.

There are something like three billion items for sale on eBay at any given moment, and one of them is sure to be exactly what you're looking for. My first time on, I couldn't think of anything I wanted to look for. Finally, I typed *"Land of the Lost* lunch box" into the search engine and waited. I'd had one in the third grade, and I remembered it being very exciting. But I certainly never expected to see one again.

A moment later, however, I discovered that there was

not one, but five, *Land of the Lost* lunch boxes for sale on eBay. Five! And all at reasonable prices. I couldn't believe it. One of the relics of my youth was available for purchase, and at an asking price of only $9.99.

Inspired, I searched for a few other items. Within 15 minutes I found an entire set of Charlie's Angels dolls, the complete run of *Tiger Beat* magazine from 1974 through 1976, a copy of *Kiss Alive II,* and the Shaun Cassidy poster that used to hang over my bed. It was as if someone had raided my childhood bedroom, placed the contents in storage, and put them up for sale 25 years later.

A flurry of bids later, I had bought back many of these treasures. And once I started, I was hooked. I started spending more and more time on eBay, searching the sales for things I desperately needed. I placed bids on board games I recalled as being hours of fun, records I knew I'd listened to over and over, and trading cards of all kinds. It became an obsession. I watched the auctions I was interested in like a hawk and found myself developing intense hatreds of people who dared to bid on what I quickly came to think of as *my* belongings. I got up in the middle of the night to win auctions that closed at odd times, reveling in the rush that came when the final seconds ticked away and I emerged victorious.

Then the items I won started arriving. Box after box was brought to my door by my weary UPS man, and soon my house was filled with childhood memories. I looked fondly at things I hadn't seen in decades, feeling a wave of nostalgia wash over me as I fondled the cards from a vintage Mystery Date game, unwrapped action figures I'd thought were lost forever, and—the biggest thrill of all—

flipped through the pages of the very first issue of *Playgirl* magazine I'd ever laid eyes on and saw once again the centerfold I'd fantasized about so many times. It all seemed too good to be true.

And that's the problem. It *was* too good to be true. There I was, surrounded by all of the best parts of my golden youth. But it wasn't the same. Somehow, burying G.I. Joe up to his neck in the mud and pretending it was quicksand wasn't as thrilling as it had been when I'd done it in our backyard with my best friend, Mickey Whitola. Wearing the T-shirt with Farrah Fawcett Majors in her red bathing suit and perky nipples on it around the house didn't have the same naughty air as it did when my mother was around to be shocked. Even the *Playgirl* centerfold had lost his charm, his feathered hair and Pearl Drops smile failing to arouse lust in my heart the way they had when we'd first met.

I think I liked it better when things that went out of my life *stayed* out of it. Memory is a tricky thing. People and events change over time. You leave out the icky bits and you make the OK parts into something more magical than they really were. Or maybe they *were* magical, but only in that particular place and time. There are things I remember—or at least think I remember—from my childhood that are very clear: the smell of the Sears Christmas catalog, the taste of the bubble gum in a package of baseball cards, the way the little plastic pegs in a Lite-Brite glowed like jewels when you turned it on.

These things all made me very happy once upon a time. But I'm afraid if I had the chance to experience them again now, they would just seem ordinary. I'd find out that they really weren't as great as I thought they were, the same way I was disappointed when they started rerunning *Eight Is Enough* and I realized how awful it was. One more lovely memory shot down. I'd like to keep the ones I have left, before my entire childhood is revealed as the barren wasteland it apparently was.

After experiencing the letdown of the *Land of the Lost* lunch box and the *Playgirl*, I called my sister and performed a little experiment. "Do you remember the time when we were kids and we spent that rainy Saturday afternoon watching *Yellow Submarine* on television and making Jiffy Pop popcorn in the fireplace?" I asked.

She groaned. "Oh, that was awful," she said. "Don't you remember how we burned our fingers on that stupid aluminum foil and half the kernels didn't pop anyway? And it wasn't *Yellow Submarine*. It was *Heidi*."

"Oh, right," I said. "But how about when we used to go to Dairy Queen for those ice cream cones covered in the crunchy cherry shell? *That* was cool."

"No, it wasn't," she shot back. "They always dripped down your hand and then Dad yelled at us about getting it on the seats."

"Did we grow up in the same family?" I asked sullenly.

"You know what *was* cool, though?" my sister said. "Going to the pool."

"God, it was so *not* cool," I responded. "We always came back with bright red eyes and horrible sunburns, and half the time Mom forgot to come get us and we had to ride home with that weird woman down the street whose kids always smelled like Clorox."

My sister sighed. "Whatever," she said.

I've noticed that my friends who collect things rarely collect things that belonged to the era they actually lived in as children. They'll collect things like comic books from the 1950s or cigarette ads from the 1920s or Pee-wee Herman dolls from the 1980s, but they seldom collect anything they might actually have played with. I think this is because, deep down, we know the associations we have with the artifacts of our childhoods are probably false, or at least tinted with the rosy glow of distance, much like the faces of the celebrities who grace the cover of *Vanity Fair* are airbrushed to perfection so we can trick ourselves into believing that they really do live in a place where no one has acne or puffy eyes. We can safely gather objects from other people's childhoods because we have no actual memories of them and we can idealize the times out of which they came. But when we start putting the playthings *we* handled around us, they look back at us with uneasy expressions and we begin to suspect that maybe things weren't quite as we remember them.

Still, it's fun to look from time to time to see what other memories are for sale on eBay. For the most part, I'm able to resist the urge to buy them and just enjoy the memories—however false they may be—that seeing them again brings back. Just keep your hands off the Easy-Bake Oven. I saw it first.

Private Parts

I've been thinking a lot about penises lately.

Actually, I've been thinking about vaginas too.

More and more, I feel as if we're all being defined by the parts of our bodies that reside between our legs. Really, it's as if the very center of civilization can be found in those few square inches of skin and hair.

A couple of things got me started on this train of thought. One is the fuss over gay marriage and the ongoing battle surrounding gay rights in general. Think about it—why are people afraid of homosexuality? It's not because we make better pasta salads or have wittier comebacks. It's because the idea of two women or two men getting it on upsets them. Have you ever been in a theater during a movie in which two men kissed? If so, you've heard the nervous titters and even the outright booing.

The fact is, people who find homosexuality disturbing generally do so because they can't stand the thought of one man putting another man's dick in his mouth or of one woman putting her tongue in another woman's pussy. Why? Most straight men would kill to have a woman suck their dicks. And straight women are forever complaining that the men in their lives don't know how to give oral sex. So what difference does it make if the body attached to the head that's doing the sucking or licking has a penis or a vagina? It's just a tongue licking a lot of skin cells and nerve endings.

But for some reason it does matter.

We put a lot of importance on our private parts and their biological uses. The whole defense of marriage thing is essentially about defining marriage as a union between someone with a vagina and someone with a penis. Why? It's not as if every marriage—or even every act of sex— results in pregnancy. So who cares what genitals two people have? Since when are relationships primarily about rubbing genitalia together anyway? Basically, what the DOMA dummies are saying is that emotional commitment and daily interaction take a back seat to the ability to insert Tab A into Slot B.

Of course, it's easy to say that it's only straight people—specifically, homophobic ones—who have this obsession with genitalia. But it's not just them. Just ask any gay man when was the last time he fantasized about Pamela Anderson going down on him. Which brings me to the other thing that has me stewing over naughty bits. See, over the past couple of years several of my friends have decided to undergo gender reassignment. I love that term—gender reassignment. It sounds as if you were put in the wrong homeroom on the first day of school and have to switch from Miss Appleby's class to Mrs. Lupino's.

In general, I have this habit of thinking of people primarily as personalities encased in big fleshy costumes. I don't generally relate to my friends in terms of male and female. They're just my friends. But now that some of them are switching from being boy friends to girl friends, and others from girl friends to boy friends, I've been thinking about it a little more. And in the end I keep coming up with the same question: "Will that make him/her gay or straight now?"

Take my friend Dirk. Dirk used to be my friend Darcy. Darcy was a lesbian separatist who didn't want anything to do with penises. Then she went and turned herself into Dirk. That part I got right away. But then Dirk started dating men. Gay men. And just to make things really interesting, he never did get rid of the thing that made him Darcy in the first place. That's right, he still has his girl plumbing. He says he likes having it and never wanted to get rid of it. He just wanted to be a boy. But without the penis. To me that's kind of like having chocolate cake without the chocolate, but it's her life. I mean his.

Anyway, now Darcy is Dirk but he has a she's parts, and he doesn't have sex with girls anymore but only does it with guys, and only gay guys and not guys who usually like the parts that girls have. This is because he says that he was queer when he was a she and he's still queer now that she's a he, so he has to sleep with guys or else he'd be betraying the community and wouldn't be able to live with himself. I don't know what that makes the gay guys who like having sex with his her-parts, but there you are. All I know is that I'm confused. I need a flow chart or something to keep it straight. I mean orderly.

I'm trying, but it's not easy. Most recently, my lesbian friend Janice announced that she was becoming Tom. By now this was all old hat to me, and I didn't blink an eye. Janice also announced that Tom was going to continue a relationship with Janice's girlfriend, Pamela.

"So," I said, wanting to be perfectly clear about everything in case there was a test later on, "are you still lesbians, or are you straight now?"

"Pamela is still lesbian-identified, but I'm straight," Janice said confidently. "Or Tom is anyway."

"But Pamela is going to stay with you?" I asked, making sure.

"That's right," Pamela said happily. "It doesn't matter to me what parts she has. I mean he has."

"Doesn't that sort of negate the whole lesbian thing?" I asked carefully.

They both sighed. "People are more than pronouns and sexual organs," Janice said, as if talking to a five-year-old.

That's all well and good—in theory. After all, it's what I was going on about earlier. But the fact is, all of these gender changes *are* about pronouns and sexual organs. That's why they're gender changes and not a drawn-out game of Let's Pretend. I want to make sure we're all playing by the same rules here, so it's disconcerting not to know who—or what—people are. When people ask me if Tom (who used to be Janice) is a lesbian, I have to stop and think for a minute. Things are further complicated by the fact that Janice is still in the process of becoming Tom. That means to some people she's still Janice and a lesbian, while to others he's Tom and isn't. When discussing Janice/Tom I have to constantly juggle those gender indicators or resort to saying "they" because English has no neuter pronouns, a grammatical obstacle that has always annoyed the writer in me.

When it gets really tricky is when one of my friends is romantically interested in one of my other friends who has been through a gender change. When my friend Adam announced that he thought my friend Kate was really hot, I wondered if I needed to tell him that Kate used to be Sam. Was it important? Kate no longer has Sam's parts, but did Adam have a right to know that his dream girl used to belong to the part of the population in which he'd never displayed a romantic interest? Would it matter to him that Kate's innie used to be an outie? I really didn't know, but it seemed sort of stupid to drag up the whole "she used to be a he" thing when the point of Sam becoming Kate was to leave all that behind. I mean, we're not supposed to mention that Traci Lords did porn now that she's a serious actress, right? So why go digging up the past about this little thing? Ultimately I didn't say anything and let Kate tell him herself. Ironically, Kate then told Adam she couldn't date him because he wasn't Jewish. So now he's going to classes at her temple, and if everything works out, they're going to be what they're calling a fully converted couple.

When I was a kid—not all that long ago—changing your gender was a big deal. Two or three times a year, Donahue did shows about it, which I watched with a mixture of fascination and puzzlement. Now Ricki and Leeza and Sally do shows about it every other day and no one blinks an eye, not even the people who are finding out their high school prom dates are now the same gender they themselves are. Or were. I have at least a dozen friends who are no longer the gender they were at birth, and it doesn't seem at all unusual any more. I know, that seems like a lot. Even I was surprised when I counted them up. I guess I just hang out at the right places.

I'd really like to think that the whole genital thing doesn't matter so much. But I don't think that's true. If my lover came to me one day and announced that he wanted to become female, I'm not sure what my reaction would be. He'd still be the same person I fell in love with, with the same sense of humor and the same annoying habits and the same ability to make me not take myself so seriously all the time. But would I still want to have sex with him? I don't know. I'm really fond of his dick. Even though it doesn't define who he is to me, it plays a crucial role in our life together. Would that life be the same if one or the other of us suddenly found ourselves with a different bit of flesh down there?

As children, we learn fairly quickly that the primary difference between boys and girls is what we have between our legs. Unfortunately, we don't get very far beyond that as we grow up. There's a mysterious fascination with genitalia. Maybe it's because we can't find any other way to define the differences between women and men. Instead, we distill everything down to whether we pee standing up or sitting down. Then we use that distinction to make up all kinds of rules about other aspects of our lives.

I wish we could be more honest about that. Just once, I'd like to hear an antigay politician or religious leader say what really bothers him about queers. Instead of this nonsense about children needing to be raised by mothers and fathers because each gender provides children with different kinds of support, I want to hear a supporter of an antigay initiative say, "I don't think gay people should adopt children because I think it's really gross that one man puts his cock in another man's ass." And I'd probably be more likely to respect a church leader who said, "I condemn homosexuality because I think the only thing that a penis should go into is a vagina," rather than trying to obscure the issue by talking about misunderstood and distorted biblical teachings.

At the same time, I think a lot of us in the queer community need to reexamine our own ideas about these things. Penises. Vaginas. Is that all we add up to? In the minds of a lot of people it is. Maybe things would be easier if, like Barbie and G.I. Joe, we all just had little smooth plastic bumps. Then we could move on and address the things that really make us individuals.

But it wouldn't be nearly as much fun.

TIME

Time does not heal all wounds. This is one of the great lies of the modern age. Just ask the Jews, who are still smarting over the whole "wandering in the desert" thing. Or the African-Americans, who can hardly be expected to shake off that little slavery incident simply because it didn't happen yesterday. Or, perhaps most tellingly, women, who really haven't quite gotten around to seeing the humor in being blamed for the invention of sin.

Or, if you will, take me. True, I have not been cast out of my homeland, sold to the highest bidder, or christened the destroyer of Eden. But I can hold a grudge with the best of them. I refuse to accept the notion that just because something happened a long time ago—even if it was before I was born or had absolutely nothing to do with me—that I'm not entitled to be pissed off about it.

This is particularly true when it comes to relationships, where I have repeatedly demonstrated that I am fully capable of resenting my partner's past even when it occurred years before I came on the scene. Now, I am a reasonable person, and I truly do believe that what my boyfriend did before he met me has absolutely nothing to do with me. Really, I believe this. After all, I tell myself, he didn't even *know* me. I didn't know *him*. There's no reason at all that what transpired between him and anyone else should bother me in the slightest.

But it does. And this is where the whole time problem

comes in. More than once, when discussing the past—or, more precisely, my annoyance over someone else's past— someone has very reasonably said to me, "But that was a long time ago." This is true. However, it was not a long time ago for *me*. It was moments ago. It is new information. The fact that it happened to *you* one, five, or 10 years ago is not the point; the point is that for me, it is recent history. And I don't like it.

Take, for example, the unpleasant issue of one-night stands. Now, we've all had them. This is simply a fact—ugly as it may be—of gay life. No man can be expected to have gone his entire adult life without having occasionally ended up in bed with someone he chose not to ever see again. This does not, however, mean that I want to be made aware of it. Nor does it mean that just because it happened before I came along—perhaps even many years before— that I am going to receive the news of its having happened with anything approaching calm acceptance.

No, I am going to be irritable about it. Very irritable. Irrationally irritable. Because the fact is, it wasn't *me* my partner had the one-night stand with. It was someone else. And that is not a good thing. This is particularly true if the one-night stand happens to be unattractive, because the inevitable thought that *naturally* arises is not *I'm so glad my boyfriend is with me now* but *What the hell was he thinking, and what does it say about* me?

It has been explained to me again and again by people much more mentally well than myself that this is not a rational position to take. As if I don't know that already. Those who attempt to convince me of this simply don't understand, though, that this is a situation that defies logic. This isn't about being rational. I've never claimed to be rational. This is about being deliriously irrational. It's about having something to poke at, like a loose tooth or a scab. It feels good, in a weird way, to work on it for a while. Eventually I'll get bored and move on to something else, but for the moment I'm having a good time.

I have a friend whose first lover was a notorious cheater. After several years of this, my friend finally dumped the jerk and moved on. Recently he let it slip that the two of them were talking again after almost seven years of not speaking.

"Why?" I asked instantly. "After what he did?"

"That was a long time ago," my friend said. "I'm over it."

Over it. This is not a concept I understand. "But you wanted to kill him when you walked in on him with that guy!" I protested.

My friend laughed, as if this was funny. "I'll never forget the look on his face," he said. "It was priceless."

"I can't believe you," I said, stunned. "This man *cheated* on you, and you're talking about it like it's no big deal."

"It's not a big deal anymore," said my friend. "Like I said, that was a long time ago."

No. Absolutely not. It may have *happened* a long time ago, but it happened. The fact that this guy was in bed with someone else, having sex, does not change just because 2,534 days have passed. The fact that he was in bed with someone else, having sex, does not change just because my friend has lived in three cities, buried a dog, eaten 7,436 meals, and slept with probably 16 other guys since then. It still happened.

I have another friend who wants to know all about his

boyfriends' pasts. He wants then to describe their exes and what they did in bed. He wants to know everything, from hair color to dick size to favorite position.

I love my friend dearly, but sometimes I wish for bad things to happen to him. "Why shouldn't I know?" he says. "It has nothing to do with me."

"Bah!" I cry when he does this, all of the horror I'm experiencing reduced to this primal sound. "Bah!" I cry, grinding my teeth so hard that I can feel them cracking. *Not have anything to do with him?* How can he think this? It's too well-adjusted, too healthy. I resent having to see it live and in person. I know he's saying it just to annoy me.

I still remember slights perpetrated on me by people in preschool. (Linda Wilkerson, wherever you are, I will have you know that my drawing of a duck did *not* look like a monkey with wings. And David Sears, may you burn in hell for taking the last sheet of purple construction paper and leaving me with orange.) These memories have not faded with age, not one bit. They are still vivid, still ready for poking and prodding whenever I feel like it.

Several months ago I had a dream about a boy who tormented me in junior high school. In my dream we met by accident, and he proceeded to tell me how great it was to see me. "What are you talking about?" I asked. "You made my life miserable."

In the dream the boy looked at me, confused, and said, "What did I do? Tell me."

There I was, all set to confront him. For years I had pored over the list of his crimes against me, reliving them in exquisite detail so that when I saw him again I would be ready to enumerate them one by one. The problem was,

THE LITTLE BOOK OF NEUROSES

now I couldn't think of a single thing he'd done. I searched desperately for one of the many examples lurking in my brain. But nothing came. All I could do was stand there, staring silently.

"See," he said. "Things weren't as bad as you think they were."

Yes, they were. And I'm annoyed that I didn't get the chance to tell him exactly what I'd thought of him back then. But that's OK—there are still a lot of other things I can resent right here and now. There are former editors and my boyfriend's exes and unpleasant reviewers. There are park rangers and Republican presidents and the inventor of track lighting. Every one of them can provide hours of hostile fun. Those on the enemies list are many, and each will get a turn. Call me crazy if you want to. Just remember—I won't forget it.

Unnatural Causes

This morning I received two things in the mail. One was a clipping from *The Kansas City Star,* sent to me by a reader who thought I would find it interesting. It was an article about the frighteningly high death rate from AIDS complications among Roman Catholic priests and how for years church leaders have been covering up this fact. The second thing I received was a letter from my friend Dr. June Steffensen Hagen.

It's interesting how seemingly unrelated things take on new meaning when they're brought together. Ordinarily I might have read the *Star* article and filed it away to think about later. But then there was June.

June was one of my English professors in college. I was her assistant for two years. My job was to photocopy the endless stream of articles she clipped from *The New York Times,* manage her convoluted filing system, and wash the teacups that piled up on her desk at an alarming rate.

At a school that ran rampant with muddleheaded fundamentalist Christian teaching, June was a breath of fresh air, a fiercely intelligent, liberal Episcopalian determined to get her students to think for themselves instead of believing everything they were told. More than once she upset the powers that be, and more than a few people would have liked to see her ousted.

Knowing June changed my life. Not only did she introduce me to writers and ideas I'd never encountered, she was the first person to let me know that being gay was OK. She was also the first person I'd ever met who I think genuinely loved God. Having grown up with a lot of people who feared God or used him as a weapon, it was something of a shock to find someone who thought of God as her friend. Determined as I was because of my past experiences to believe the whole God thing was a lot of nonsense, June made me rethink that position. In fact, when it was time for me to leave school, I even applied to the Episcopal seminary. Ultimately I didn't go, which I know now was the right choice. But at the time it was an appealing option.

June's husband, Jim, is a retired Episcopal priest who for many years served a largely Spanish-speaking community in Queens. Her letter to me was filled with news about their lives: their recent trips to Ecuador and Mexico, the literature class June was teaching, her and Jim's involvement in the New York Choral Society and their parish, and the activities of their two children. These are the pieces of a full and happy life. They're what I think of when I think of June.

And then I think of those priests dying of AIDS. According to the *Star* article, many of them were sent to hospices outside of their parishes to die, alone and far from their friends and families so that no one would know what was killing them. In almost all cases, the cause of death was listed as "natural causes" and the occupation written on the death certificate was listed as anything but priest. In the end, these servants of the church were reduced to lies, their years of service to God wiped out with the stroke of a pen to protect the image of the institution to which they had devoted their lives.

Tucked into June's letter is a photograph of her and Jim, taken on one of their trips. June's hair is grayer than it was when I was her student assistant, and Jim's is more absent, but the smiles on their faces still reflect the love of life and each other that I remember. The most wonderful thing about it, though, is how much they look like a couple. Jim has his arm around June, and she's leaning into him in a way that radiates familiarity and friendship—a picture of a lifetime spent together exploring the world and all of its joys and challenges.

I can't help but compare this to the image in my head of priests dying, alone and frightened, among strangers because their superiors sent them away to hide their shame. I want to believe that someone was there to hold their hands, to tell them they were loved. I want to believe they died knowing their lives meant something. But I don't think they did. I think that in the end they were betrayed in the cruelest way.

The Episcopal Church and the Church of Rome have been at odds since the beginning, and theologians and academics can argue points of doctrine until they're blue in the face. When it comes down to it, though, the only thing that matters is how a church serves its people, and the Catholic Church gets failing marks in that department. I'm sure the church sees its dead priests as embarrassments best forgotten, the same way for years it ignored the rampant sexual and emotional abuse of young people by its clergy. What the Catholic Church should really be embarrassed about, though, is its refusal to acknowledge the needs of the men who come to it offering up their lives. In order to maintain control, they strip them of their humanity, forcing them to give up love and companionship and, yes, plain old sex in a misguided attempt at manufacturing piety. Sublimating desire in incense and robes and a rehearsed liturgy mumbled two or three times a day is a recipe for unhappiness. And for death by the most unnatural cause of all—shame.

One of the things June taught me was that God—in whatever form you embrace him—loves joy. It saddens me that the Catholic priests who came to worship God with joy were met instead with betrayal and fear in the hour when they most needed love. I am also angered—angered enough to want to comfort myself with disbelief in a God who would let this happen, just as I wanted to back in college.

But, once again, June won't let me do that. I've put the picture of her and Jim on the wall above my desk, right beside the picture of my Wiccan friend Archer dressed in a hat covered with enormous yellow roses and the one of the stone circle and phallic rock monument my Radical Faerie brother, Ron, painstakingly built on his Maine sheep farm. When I look at these pictures, I am reminded that even the fear of an institution as large and imposing as the Catholic Church is nothing compared to the power of one or two people who truly understand what it is to live with joy. And I am reminded too that God comes in many forms, that the God those priests were searching for really does exist somewhere, waiting for them. I hope they've found him.

So You Want to Be a Drag Queen

Men dressing up as women is hardly news. But doing it *well* is something else altogether. Simply throwing on any old dress and applying a little lipstick does not a drag queen make. A true drag queen possesses a rare blend of beauty, wit, and poise that elevates her to near-goddess status. Achieving this level of success takes time, patience, and a great deal of waxing. It is not an aspiration for the faint of heart or those lacking in style. So before you decide to step into those heels, take the following quiz to determine your true drag potential.

1. Which of the following personalities truly epitomizes the essence of drag:
   (a) Milton Berle
   (b) RuPaul
   (c) Barbara Bush

2. There is no such thing as too much blue eye shadow.
   (a) True
   (b) False
   (c) It depends on whether you're going for a day or evening look

3. You can always tell if a person is a drag queen or a real girl by:
   (a) The size of the hands

(b) The size of the feet

(c) The size of the hair

4. Which of the following techniques is *not* acceptable
when attempting to win a drag contest:
  (a) Replacing another girl's tape of Gloria Gaynor's "I
  Will Survive" with a tape of Bob Dylan's "Man
  Gave Names to All the Animals"
  (b) Holding a gun to a kitten's head and threatening
  to pull the trigger if you lose
  (c) Loosening the heels on another girl's shoes

5. The best way to hide your "candy" when donning a
bathing suit or other revealing outfit is to:
  (a) Tuck and tape
  (b) Nip and tuck
  (c) Cut and curl

6. Which of the following is an acceptable drag name:
  (a) Boutros Boutros-Ghali
  (b) Carmen Electra
  (c) Ivana Trailer

7. In the drag world clothes are to image as:
  (a) Paint is to house
  (b) Carats are to diamond
  (c) Water is to fish

8. When you think about putting on women's clothing
you:
  (a) Worry about someone catching you
  (b) Worry about looking stupid

(c) Worry about not being able to find navy pumps in
your size

9. Which of the following is the most important event on
television:
   (a) The Miss America pageant
   (b) The Super Bowl
   (c) The Westminster Dog Show

10. The best thing to put on your hair is:
    (a) Conditioner
    (b) Miss Clairol
    (c) A tiara

ANSWERS:

1. (b)
2. (a)
3. (c)
4. (b)
5. (a)
6. (c)
7. (b)
8. (c)
9. (a)
10. (c)

SCORING:

Give yourself five points for each correct answer.

0–10: You are probably too hopeless—and hairy—to attain

drag queen status. Stick to being a member of the audience. After all, we can't all be doers.

15–20: It was sort of cute when you dressed up like Patsy Cline for Halloween, but really, once a year is probably enough.

25–30: You understand that drag is far more than just camp. But are you willing to let your Inner Queen emerge into the spotlight?

35–40: You're *so* close. All you need is a little coaching from someone more skilled in the art of drag and you'll be on your way. Find a fairy godmother to help you transform yourself.

45–50: A diva in waiting. If you haven't already heard the sound of a Halston dress whispering your name, you soon will. Prepare to ascend your throne and be worshiped as the queen you are.

How I Got This Way, or,
Did *Tiger Beat* Make Me Gay?

A couple of weeks ago I was in line at the post office, standing behind a woman with three boys. One was a baby. He sat in his stroller looking out at everything with wide, interested eyes while he blew spit bubbles and laughed at the miracle of his own tiny fingers. The oldest boy was probably 9 or 10. He slumped at the counter where the change of address forms and mailing labels were arranged, systematically spreading the neat piles into a chaotic mess while restlessly shuffling from foot to foot as his mother periodically told him to stop making a mess.

The third boy, who looked to be about 7, stood quietly beside his mother. Like his older brother, he was dressed in shorts and a T-shirt. But where his brother had on a pair of lived-in tennis shoes, the middle boy's feet were encased in sandals. This in itself wouldn't have been so remarkable if his toenails hadn't been painted in glittery pink polish.

For a moment I thought perhaps it wasn't a little boy at all. But a more concentrated inspection confirmed that indeed it was. It also confirmed that not only were his toenails painted, but so were his fingernails—in the same glittery pink polish. Other than that, he looked like any other 7-year-old boy.

The line was moving *very* slowly, so I had a long time

to observe the mother and boys. The baby really wasn't very interesting once the spitting and laughing routine got old, and the older boy seemed to possess a disturbing but ultimately futile dedication to single-handedly upending the entire United States Postal Service organizational system, such as it is. What did fascinate me, though, was how none of the other family members seemed the slightest bit concerned about the middle boy's polish wearing. Perhaps, I thought, they were so used to it that they didn't even notice it anymore. But *that* implied that this was not an isolated incident, that he must do it on a regular enough basis that it had become routine. If that was the case, then it raised all kinds of other questions, like what did his father think about it, when had the boy first started doing it, and—most intriguing of all—who was it exactly who bought the polish for him.

The more I looked at the little boy, the more I wanted to know his story. Did he know that a lot of people might find his polish wearing strange? Did he feel self-conscious standing in the post office with his glittery toenails on display for everyone in line to gawk at? And, now that I thought of it, *were* people gawking?

I looked around to see if the boy's polish had attracted anyone else's attention. It was hard to tell. The glassy-eyed expressions on the faces of the people behind me as they looked at their watches and calculated the rapidly diminishing remainders of their lunch hours gave few clues.

Of course, what I was really wondering was whether the little boy was a queen. When I was his age, wearing nail polish would have been a dead giveaway. Nowadays, though, you can't be sure. Polish wearing seems fairly commonplace among the hipper teenage boy set. Even MTV's Carson Daly sports it from time to time.

But Carson's nail polish is black, and it's usually only on one or two nails at a time. This kid's was on every toe and every finger. And it was glittery *pink* polish. Definitely a sissy color, the kind that used to come with the strange life-size Barbie head whose hair you could cut and whose face you could make up with blue eye shadow and red lipstick. But I'm getting ahead of myself. We'll return to Barbie a little later. The point is, the little boy was wearing what could only be called *girls'* nail polish.

A moment later the mother turned to the oldest boy. "Bradley," she said, "get over here. If you manage not to destroy anything for the next five minutes, maybe we'll go next door and get ice cream when we're done."

Bradley reluctantly left the tattered scraps of return receipts and delivery notification slips and went to stand beside his mother. His brother, however, came to life in glorious fabulousness. It was as if his mother had sprinkled magic pixie dust over his head and released his inner queen. He flailed his glittery hands around and said excitedly, "Oh, goody. Ice cream! Can I get those little sprinkles on top? I *love* those little sprinkles."

I am not making this up. The kid was so excited and waving his hands around so excitedly that I thought he might fly away. His mother, still seemingly oblivious to his behavior, merely nodded. The little boy turned to Bradley. "Did you hear that?" he said, clutching his hands to his chest. "We're getting *ice cream.*"

"I *heard* her," said Bradley, rolling his eyes. "Why do you get so excited over *everything?*"

At that point the clerk called out "Next!" and the mother pushed the stroller toward the service window. Bradley and his brother dutifully followed, Bradley once again looking bored and his brother still gushing about sprinkles and ice cream. As I watched them walk away I wanted to call out, "You go, girl!"

I wanted to say the same thing to the mother and to Bradley, because I was just as impressed with how they reacted to the little polish-wearing boy as I was with how comfortable he seemed to be with his little gay self. Sure, Bradley had been a little bit irritable about his brother's enthusiasm for the sprinkles, but it's the same way I react to the dog when he barks at the telephone for the 38th time in an afternoon. Let's face it, misplaced zeal *can* be a little trying.

Maybe the kid got away with the pink polish because he's young, and no one expects him to really know any better. Or maybe it's his attitude. I suspect the little boy didn't think there was anything odd about it at all. If he had, I don't think he would have been able to carry it off. Instead, I think he just thought it was fun. But this raises the larger question: What makes some of us want to put on fingernail polish in the first place? Which, of course, is just another way of asking two *really big* questions: Why are some of us gay, and when do we know?

The why part is the more difficult to answer, so we'll start with the when. When did you know you were gay? Most of us have been asked that question at least once, and usually many times. I myself was asked it very recently while serving as the lone queer on a radio talk show panel. "Well," I answered thoughtfully, "I suppose it was when I dreamt about the father on *Flipper* taking me camping and asking me to share his sleeping bag."

This is not, technically, true. I did fantasize about the dad from *Flipper*. But the real answer is that I don't remember ever *not* knowing. At the very least, I don't remember a time when I ever thought about ending up with a girl. I just never actually had a name for it, not until junior high when the words "faggot" and "fairy" were mentioned in conjunction with my name. Even then I didn't see what the big deal was, although it certainly wasn't a lot of fun being singled out for being different.

What I *do* remember is liking my friend Stephanie's Easy-Bake Oven, and the pictures of Shaun Cassidy taped over her bed, and her life-size Barbie head, which I think was called Cut-N-Curl Barbie. It came with eye shadow and blush and real curlers, and you could make up Barbie's face and do her hair. I was never very good at it, and poor Barbie always came out looking like some kind of trailer park whore, but it was fun nonetheless. So was making little cakes in the Easy-Bake Oven. Stephanie and I used to spend long afternoons in her Holly Hobbie–decorated bedroom playing with these things and having a wonderful time. It never occurred to me that other boys might not be doing the same thing.

If it bothered my parents that I was doing these things, they never said anything. I also liked big butch Tonka trucks (which is probably where my love of blue-collar men came from), electric race car sets (which is probably where my love of guys who are into fast cars came from), and sending my G.I. Joe on all kinds of dangerous missions (which is probably where my love of military men came from). It may have helped that the Easy-

Bake Oven and Cut-N-Curl Barbie head remained out of their sight, safe in Stephanie's bedroom, so perhaps they never even noticed. Only once did they do anything that might have indicated some possible worries on their part, and that was when, for Christmas when I was 8, they presented me with a set of weights. I'd been hoping for a Lite-Brite, so I was more than a little irritated. But I feigned excitement, and they seemed relieved.

While I never received an Easy-Bake Oven of my own, other eccentricities were indulged without comment. No one blinked when, like Stephanie, I bought a poster of Shaun Cassidy and hung it over my bed. I also bought his records ("That's Rock and Roll" was the first 45 single I ever purchased) and played them on the tinny little turntable I'd inherited from one of my sisters. And, perhaps most important, I bought every single issue of *Tiger Beat* magazine and read it cover to cover.

Which brings us, naturally, to the second big question: Why are some of us gay? I'm sure it was *Tiger Beat* that made me gay or at least finalized the process. Looking back, I realize the magazine was basically *Playgirl* without the nudity. Every issue was crammed with photos of the hunks of the 1970s, and nearly every one of them was shirtless. There was Shaun, of course, and his brother David. Then there was Leif Garrett, the Bay City Rollers, Donny Osmond, and that kid from *James at 15*. Occasionally there would be photos of the guys from Kiss and the Village People. I liked these best of all, because they showed chest hair, and for a time I had a recurring dream about Paul Stanley of Kiss and the construction worker from the Village People coming to my house for a sleepover.

This brings up an interesting issue. Was I attracted to the guys in *Tiger Beat* because I was queer, or did a constant diet of them push me in that direction? Ultimately, I don't really care. But I sincerely doubt that looking at pictures of Shaun and the Village People's leatherman caused anything that wasn't already hardwired into my psyche. After all, I also had pictures of Jaclyn Smith and Farrah Fawcett on my walls, but I never dreamed about them. I watched *Charlie's Angels* because it was fun; I watched *Adam-12* because seeing the guys in uniform made me wish they would come over and rescue me from some imminent peril. Particularly if they brought their handcuffs and nightsticks. But that's another story.

So, *Tiger Beat* or fate? As I said, I think it's just the luck of the draw. But let's consider the other side. What if there *are* other determining factors? Certainly some people think there are, like those "ex-gay" folks and Dr. Laura. Just to humor them—and in the interest of scientific fairness—let's examine some of the more popular "causes" of homosexuality.

1. The distant father/smothering mother. This is a nice idea. After all, it ties up a lot of psychological issues into one neat package. But really, how many of us—straight or gay—*didn't* have distant fathers and overbearing mothers to one extent or another? That was their *job* back then, before we were all enlightened and New Aged and therapied into familial bliss. *Eight Is Enough* aside, most of our parents fell into this category, so I hardly think it's fair to pin everything on them. Besides, how come one smothering mother might produce a tennis

prodigy while another produces a boy who can sit through the entire *Ring Cycle* and love it? With such varying results, the evidence is spotty at best.

2. Not playing sports. Sports were a big deal when I was a kid. Little League baseball and Pop Warner football were *the* thing. Most of my friends played one or both. I didn't play either. While today, I love baseball, I never wanted to play it when I was 10. I hated gym class, and I despised anything resembling athletic competition. But I know a lot of gay men who loved playing sports, even the ones where you have to tackle other people and sweat a lot. I didn't dislike sports because I was a baby queer, I disliked them because I didn't want to be around other people any more than I absolutely had to. I don't play well with others. I never have. The idea of being on a *team* was horrifying to me then and still is. I think the only thing teamwork prepares you for is being a Republican.

3. Dressing up in your mom's clothes. Given the fact that the majority of transvestites are straight men, I don't think we can give any credibility to the notion that putting on some women's clothing at the age of 6 might flip a switch in a kid's brain and make him a fag. Let's face it—men's clothing is boring. We have pants and we have shirts. But women get all kinds of cool stuff, so of course their clothes are more fun to wear. I don't think putting on your best friend's mother's bra and chasing him through the

house is the beginning of a lifestyle. However, given the fact that some of our community insist on wearing things like capri pants and nipple-revealing tank tops, I might have to reconsider this.

Those seem to be the big three. While interesting concepts, none of them really seem candidates for turning a kid queer. I think *Tiger Beat* is much more likely to do that, or perhaps all of that sugar most of us ate as kids. Maybe we should blame it all on Pixie Stix or the gum that came in *Star Wars* trading cards. I, for one, consumed enough Hostess products to produce an entire gay men's chorus, and I wouldn't be at all surprised to find out that something in them altered my brain chemistry. But ultimately, I think some of us are just meant to be gay.

Still, it annoys me when people argue that it must be biological because no one would *choose* to be gay. I sure would. I love being gay, especially the part where I get to sleep with men. I wouldn't go straight for all the money in the world. I wouldn't go straight even if it meant ending world hunger, war, and the razing of the Amazon rain forest. If tomorrow someone came up with a patch or pill or shot that would make me straight, I'd stubbornly refuse to take it. I'm gay because I was made that way, but I definitely *choose* to enjoy it.

So maybe we won't ever know whether homosexuals are born or made. Having said that, let's look further at the question we *can* answer with more authority—when do you know? As I said earlier, I pretty much always knew, even if it took me a while to have a word for it. But I have friends who didn't have a clue. Two of my lesbian friends didn't figure it out until they were in their mid 30s and living together as roommates. One day they just woke up in their separate bedrooms and simultaneously thought, *Gosh, we must be dykes.* They've been together ever since.

The world is filled with stories like this—men and women who take a while to discover their gay selves. Some of them try being straight, perhaps getting married and having children first. Others wander around in a daze, wondering why things seem just a little bit confusing. But that's OK. There's no rush. As long as you get to the party eventually, you're fine. However, it's sometimes nice to have some help, so for those who might not be sure of their sexuality, I offer here a few handy hints.

THE TOP 10 CLUES THAT YOU MIGHT BE A GAY MAN

1. When someone asks you if you're a pitcher or a catcher, your first thought isn't about baseball.

2. When you see a handsome police officer following you on the highway, you speed up instead of slowing down.

3. You've wondered if Batman and Robin share a bedroom.

4. Your idea of "getting lucky" on the weekend is finding Ralph Lauren sheets on sale.

5. You're best friends with the girl you took to your high school prom.

6. You noticed that Ricky Martin shaved his chest for his last video.

7. You're the one everyone turns to when they need someone to plan a surprise party.

8. You own moisturizer that has to be bought at a cosmetics counter.

9. You can recite the next line of the following song: "The minute you walked in the joint, I could see you were a man of distinction."

10. When viewing straight porn videos you watch the women give head and think, *They're not doing that right.*

The Top 10 Clues That You Might Be a Lesbian

1. Whenever you hear an acoustic guitar you want to cry.

2. Your idea of the perfect vacation involves a tent.

3. You have the *Vanity Fair* photo of k.d. lang getting shaved by Cindy Crawford taped to your refrigerator.

4. You get the in-jokes on *Xena.*

5. You secretly understand what your male colleagues see in playing golf.

6. You've worn out more than two food processors making hummus.

7. When you follow a guy at the gym on a piece of

equipment you add weight to what he was lifting.

8. You remember exactly what you were doing when you heard that the U.S. women's soccer team won the 1999 Women's World Cup.

9. You have cats named any of the following: Melissa, Martina, Indigo, Lily, Eleanor, Ellen, or Butch.

10. You can pee standing up.

THE TOP 10 CLUES THAT YOU'RE A CHILD WHO MIGHT GROW UP TO BE A HOMOSEXUAL

1. You eat your vegetables, but only if they're accompanied by bearnaise sauce or raspberry vinaigrette.

2. Your parents consult you about what to wear on their evenings out.

3. You beg to stay up late on Oscar night.

4. You think the stage version of *The Lion King* far surpasses the Disney film.

5. You win the school spelling bee with "chiffonier."

6. Your thermos is filled with Evian.

7. When playing with male action figures you frequently have them wrestle, and when playing with female action

figures you frequently have them act out scenes from *The Women.*

8. You understand why the Wild Things in *Where the Wild Things Are* really love Max so, you know that Frog and Toad are much more than friends, and you relate to Curious George in a special way you're sure he would understand.

9. You don't understand your peers' fascination with Britney Spears, particularly when there are people like Barbra, Bette, and Ella to listen to.

10. You can't wait until you have to take showers in gym class.

Keep in mind that these are just hints. Obviously there will be variations on all of these themes. Just like snowflakes, no two queers are alike. Some of us were in the drama club, while others played hockey. Some of us rocked to Joan Jett, while others stood in front of the mirror lip-synching to songs from *Cats.* And some of us did all of these things. But however we started out, at some point we figured out that we weren't playing on the same team as most of the world, and that changed our lives.

Take the little boy with the glittery pink nail polish. Let's assume for a moment that he *is* a budding queen. When will he know? Does he already suspect that he's somehow different from his friends? Does he understand that, as a rule, little boys do not wear glittery pink polish on their fingers and toes? Does he care? He didn't seem to, and that was the truly wonderful thing about him. He was just being himself, and from what I could see, his mother and brother were perfectly happy to let him.

A couple of years ago, I wrote about my nephew, who displayed a distinct love of show tunes. I, along with many readers, wondered if in fact Jack would turn out to be a big homo. Well, he didn't. At least I don't think he has. But if he *had*, we would all have been happy about it (some of us more than others). The point being, my sister didn't worry about it, and neither did Jack. And that's how it ought to be.

But of course it isn't. Having a gay child is still something to get all excited about for most people. Many parents, faced with a little boy who wanted to wear pink nail polish, would fall to pieces. Worse, they'd make the boy feel that his desire was something to be ashamed of. I doubt that more than a handful would actually take him to the post office with his glittery pink hands and feet on display for everyone to see.

I wonder what that little boy's mother was thinking. Was she simply focused on mailing her package and getting out of there? Or did she think about what might be in her boy's future? Did she imagine him a dozen or so years from then, meeting another guy who also wore pink nail polish as a little boy and falling in love? Did she wonder what her son's lover might be like, the way many parents imagine their daughters' future husbands and their sons' future wives? Did she think about how she'd like their commitment ceremony to be?

Probably she didn't. She had a lot of other things to think about. But maybe later, when she got the three boys home and had some time to herself, she did think about what would happen to that little boy with the glittery pink nail polish. And when she did, maybe she didn't care *why* he wanted to wear nail polish. Maybe she just hoped that someday he would be as happy with his life as he was when he heard that there was ice cream in his future.

You go, girl. Both of you.

COMMUNITY SPIRIT

I watched *The Sixth Sense* not so long ago, and I have something to tell that spooky little kid: I see dead people too. Well, OK, I don't see them. But I got an apartment once because of one.

When I first moved to Boston, my then-roommate and I moved into what seemed like a lovely apartment. And it *was* lovely, except for the fact that the woman who lived above us liked to have parties that began on Friday afternoon and lasted until approximately five minutes before she had to go to work on Monday morning. I am not exaggerating when I say that during those periods at least 300 of her closest friends came to call, and all of them wore clogs.

After three weekends of this, we couldn't stand it anymore. On a Sunday morning a week before Christmas I called Steve, the realtor who'd rented the place to us, and told him that we had to get out of there, and fast.

Twenty minutes later Steve and I were standing in the middle of an absolutely gorgeous apartment. It had everything I wanted in a home and was in fact much nicer—and cheaper—than the apartment I'd rented a few weeks before.

"I don't get it," I said as I looked at the beautiful hardwood floors and the original moldings around the fireplace. "Why didn't you show me this the last time I was looking?"

Steve made a vague gesture. "It just became available," he said.

The tone of his voice suggested there was more to the story than what he was telling me. I pressed him, asking why a prime apartment had suddenly come on the market at a very reasonable price and hadn't been snatched up yet in a town where broom closets were renting for $1,200 a month.

"All right," he said, giving in. "I didn't want to mention this because it's scared away everyone who's looked at the place, but the previous tenant killed himself."

"Here?" I asked.

Steve nodded. "In the bedroom."

I wasn't particularly bothered by this. And even if I had been, the lower rent, original moldings, and fact that the upstairs neighbors did not have 300 clog-wearing friends more than made up for any misgivings I might have had about possible bad luck hanging around. Besides, I'd happened to bring the dog with me to see the apartment, and he was running madly from room to room, which I took as a good sign. Steve and I went back to the office and signed the lease.

About five minutes after I'd handed over the deposit check, a young straight couple came into the office and told Steve they would take the place he'd showed them earlier in the week.

"Sorry," Steve said, pointing at me. "He just got it."

"I hope the ghost doesn't bother you," the young woman said. "We normally wouldn't even consider that place, but there's nothing else available."

As it turned out, five different couples—all of them

straight—had considered and rejected the apartment because of the suicide. And all five called Steve that Sunday afternoon saying they'd changed their minds and wanted it.

At first I assumed this was just a coincidence—a lot of superstitious people who had passed up a great apartment for no good reason. But then I found out a little bit more about the previous tenant of my new home.

His name was Richard, and he was gay. A few years earlier, he'd discovered that he was HIV-positive. This threw him into a depression, which worsened when his lover left him. Angry, frightened, and lonely, Richard ended his life by drinking a bottle of whiskey and hanging himself.

No one in the house knew he was dead. They saw him so seldom anyway that his presence wasn't missed. He was found only when a suicide letter he'd written and posted to one of his friends, a lesbian who lived across the street, arrived and she came over to check on him.

Richard's family had come and taken away most of his belongings, but when I moved into the apartment I discovered they'd left a lot of things behind in the basement. Going through them, I was able to piece together the fragments of his life. I found a box containing his high school yearbooks and was able to see what he looked like. I found an envelope of photographs he'd saved of himself, his friends, and his lovers. In all of these pictures he was smiling and happy.

There were other things too. Three different Monopoly games, which I later learned he used to force his friends to play whenever they came over. Boxes of

records, mostly disco and jazz. The hat he wore as a con-
ductor on Amtrak.

The yearbook and photos I gave to his friend across
the street, in case Richard's family wanted them back. The
board games, moldy from being in the basement, I threw
out except for the little metal playing pieces, which I gave
to the woman who lived above us to use in one of her art
installations. The hat I gave to another of Richard's friends
who lived on the block.

But I kept some of his things. Dishes, mostly, particularly a set of soup bowls I found in the kitchen cabinets.
And I used them. Shortly after I moved in, I did a cleansing ritual suggested by one of my witch friends. I lit can-
dles and burned sage. I sat and I thought about Richard
and the things that had driven him to take his own life.
And I ate soup out of one of his bowls.

I knew Richard only from what his friends on the
street told me, and from what I could gather from the
things he'd left behind. But he still felt like family to me. I
understood the feelings that led him to believe he couldn't
remain alive struggling with them anymore. I understood
him as a gay man. And I understood why it was important
that he not be forgotten, simply swept out of his last home
like so much dirt.

It occurred to me then that maybe Richard had been
waiting for someone to come along whom he wanted to
have living in his home. Perhaps seeing all those straight
couples walking through his rooms and looking into his
closets made him uneasy. Maybe, just maybe, he'd been
waiting for a couple of queers to come along and make a
home in the place he'd left behind.

I lived in that apartment for five years. During that time, nothing particularly odd happened. At least not to me. My roommate, who slept in what was Richard's bedroom, had a period during which he dreamed about Richard quite frequently. And from time to time, doors shut for no apparent reason or the dog stared at something no one else saw and wagged his tail. But I hardly think the place was haunted. Richard did leave traces of himself behind—like the hideous pink color he painted one of the rooms—but whatever sadness he felt, he took with him.

I like to remember Richard. I like to know that a gay man lived in my apartment. It saddens me to think that he died unhappily, but I still see him as a link in the chain, and I think keeping his memory alive makes that chain stronger. I was happier in that place than in any place I'd ever lived, and I have Richard to thank for that. Every morning when I opened the huge windows that filled the house with light, I hoped that somehow it made what he went through a little less terrible.

When I moved out of that apartment and came to California, I again found a living space in a roundabout way. The house found me, really. Again, I love the space, and being here has made me incredibly happy. But about a month after moving in, I found out that this place too was the scene of tragedy, this time involving the singer of a now-famous rock band. Before his band achieved the fame they now enjoy, this unhappy young man overdosed on heroin, leaving behind a wife, a baby, and his band mates. He never got to see what he became. The rest of the band moved out of the house, and the new owners fixed it up, covering over the old paint, repairing the scarred wooden floors, and restoring the house to its original Craftsman glory. I have yet to discover what, if anything, remains of the young man and his sadness. But sometimes when I'm sitting at my desk writing, I think about him and wonder if some of the frustration and joy I feel as part of the creative process comes from somewhere outside myself.

Memory has a way of healing, and as a community we as gay people have lost a great deal in the last decade and a half. We can't forget those we've lost. We need to remember them and what they gave to us. Because when it's all said and done, it's not the soup bowls or the Monopoly games we leave behind, it's how we are remembered by the people whose lives we touch. And maybe, if we keep remembering, we won't have to say goodbye to any more of our brothers and sisters who, like Richard, feel that they've been forgotten.

20 WAYS TO ANNOY BEAUTIFUL PEOPLE

Beautiful people (BPs) are fine in their own way. We like to see them in magazines and on movie screens, and maybe we even occasionally fantasize about being one of them or being with one of them. But let's face it—most of the time BPs are simply a gigantic pain. They suck up all the attention. They make us feel insecure. They get all the promotions, lovers, and breaks the rest of us really deserve. But fear not: There are ways to get even with the beautiful ones. With surprisingly little effort they can be put in their place, and once there they will see how the rest of us feel most of the time. Here's how.

1. Switch the tags in stores frequented by BPs so that what is really a size 32 waist is marked as a size 38.

2. When forced into conversation with a BP, comment, "It must be so hard to have everyone be totally disinterested in what you have to say."

3. At parties with lots of stylish BPs, pick the one who annoys you the most and say, "You look *exactly* like my last lover. I hope you don't age as badly as he did."

4. Tell everyone in the office that the BP promoted above you has had work done by a surgeon you know. Leave doctored "before" pictures in the copier.

5. Send the BP flowers with a note telling him to meet you that night at 7 o'clock, but don't say where and sign them "You know who."

6. Swear that the cheesecake you're serving the BP is totally fat free.

7. Ask the BP difficult questions followed immediately by, "Never mind. We don't expect you to understand these things."

8. When introduced to your recent ex's BP date, remark to the BP, "Aren't you glad he's not one of those guys who only likes gym bodies?"

9. When cut off in traffic by a BP driving an SUV or BMW, call the police with the license plate number and report the car as stolen.

10. When snubbed by a BP in a bar, tell all the ugly men that the BP digs them. Tell all the cute men that the BP has herpes.

11. Convince a BP coworker that his recently acquired Kenneth Cole shoes are last year's style. He'll worry about it all day.

12. If bored, fill out piles of magazine subscription cards in the name of the BP of your choice and check "Bill me later."

13. If sneered at by a BP, respond cheerfully with, "You may be pretty, but *I'm* the kind they marry."

14. When accosted by any uppity BP while working in a service position, respond with, "Keep it up. They don't pay me enough not to slap you."

15. When tired of hearing a BP bragging about a recent tropical vacation say, "Wow, I didn't know they made bronzer in that shade of orange."

16. Inform department store security guards that you saw a BP sticking something in his bag at the cosmetics counter.

17. When sharing a dressing room with a BP, try on all the same clothes and say, "We look just like twins!"

18. Insist that just that morning on the *Today* show, Katie Couric did a report on how moisturizer use causes brain damage in lab animals.

19. Say sincerely, "I thought only the guys in the *International Male* catalog could pull off an outfit like that, but you really make it work."

20. If the BP in question is someone famous say, "Aren't you so-and-so?" using the name of a lesser star. "Didn't you *used* to be in porn?" also works well.

WITH FRIENDS LIKE THESE

A couple of weeks ago I helped two straight boys push a car out of the snow. I was on the way to the park with the dog when I heard the unmistakable sound of tires spinning on ice. Sure enough, across the street one of the men was standing behind the car shoving while the other gunned the engine futilely. When that didn't work, the driver got out and they both stood there staring stupidly at the back tire.

I almost didn't stop. After all, these were two strapping frat-boy types. Surely they didn't need assistance. But they looked so helpless in their sweatpants and sneakers without socks, as if they'd just rolled out of bed. So I told the dog to sit and went over to offer my services.

The fellow doing all the pushing seemed surprised when I joined him behind the car, but he moved over and let me have a go at it. After more tire spinning, some forceful swearing by all of us, and one final shove, the car lurched out of its spot and the driver took off, waving to us as he turned the corner.

As I called to the dog and started to walk away, the remaining man turned to me and said awkwardly, "Well…um…thanks," before disappearing back into the house. He still seemed slightly bewildered, as if he couldn't figure out why I had stopped to help.

Since then, I've noticed something interesting.

Straight guys are funny about helping other guys. Not that they don't do it. They do. They help each other move. They help each other fix their trucks. They help each other build decks and pour foundations and whatnot. But they don't generally help guys they don't know. And when they do help each other, it almost always involves beer afterward, as if a couple hours of manly drinking makes up for the fact that they've just engaged in a cooperative endeavor.

Gay men are different. We think nothing of asking for or giving help. We help each other plan dinners and vacations. We depend on our friends to tell us when our new jeans make our ass look huge. We talk about our new loves and our old exes, and we expect our friends to come up with answers for why we haven't found the perfect guy yet.

And we don't just ask our friends. Any gay guy will do. I've been in unfamiliar cities and been able to walk up to gay men on the street and ask them where the nearest queer bookstore is. I've gotten the best workout advice from muscle queens at my gym. The other day, while I was sitting waiting for a flight, a man came up and asked me if I would watch his bag for a minute. When he returned, we spent half an hour talking about how great it is to be gay, because you can almost always find someone to hang out with when you travel alone. It's sort of like being in a gang, but with better parties.

Straight men just don't have this. They don't bond in the same way. When they get an urge to hang out with one another, they have to join the army or play sports. It's like they're afraid of being with each other unless every single minute is scheduled. Or maybe they just don't have anything to say to one another. I don't know. I just think they're weird. I especially think they're weird when they go to movies together and sit with an empty seat between them so no one will think they're on a date or anything.

Maybe the problem is that straight men don't really know how to have friends. They have guys they hang out with, guys they play ball with, guys they work with, and guys they say hello to just because they see them every morning on the way to work. But I'm not sure they actually have friends in the same way that gay men have friends.

My friend Jeff recently began dating a man who, until not very long before, was for all intents and purposes straight. One night, after Jeff and this man had dinner with some of Jeff's friends, the guy remarked to Jeff that he was really jealous of all the close friendships Jeff had. He said it had never occurred to him that men could actually be friends with other men and have relationships that spanned many years. The men in his life had always been there out of necessity or proximity, not because he wanted them there or because he shared anything special with them.

This is something a lot of us forget sometimes. Being gay, we learn to make our own families, and those families consist, by and large, of our friends. No, we don't have a monopoly on friendships. Straight people get to have friends too. But when I look at the many important friendships in my life, I can't help but notice that my parents never really had anything like them, nor do my straight siblings. Maybe they replaced friends with spouses and children and the more insular existence that marriage and family often impose on people. That makes me value my friends in relationships and my friends with children even more. Being part of their lives and having them as part of mine give me something I think a lot of folks miss out on.

And, if nothing else, I always know I have people who will help me push my car out of the snow.

ONE ON ONE

I've been thinking about cheating on my boyfriend.

I've been thinking about it since the night a few weeks ago when I was at a cocktail party without him and someone I was chatting with said, "So, which of these boys will you be going home with tonight?"

"None of them," I said. "I have a boyfriend."

My acquaintance chuckled. "So do I," he said. "But what does that have to do with anything?"

When I explained that my boyfriend and I are monogamous, I was met with a bewildered expression. My friend looked at me as if he were face-to-face with the last remaining dodo bird and wasn't quite sure if he believed it was still breathing. I think he thought I was kidding.

But I wasn't. And that seems to bother people. I've noticed that whenever the issue of monogamy comes up in conversation, people get a little edgy. Tell them that you and your lover are faithful, and they start trying to prove that you're lying. It's like being audited by the IRS. Suddenly everything is suspect, and you're expected to come up with receipts and canceled checks as evidence to support your claim.

Monogamy as aberrant behavior is something I never really considered. I've just always been wired that way. But apparently a lot of my gay brothers aren't. The more I talk to my friends, both in and out of relationships, the more I discover that a lifetime of sex with one person isn't everyone's idea of a good time. For many of the men I know, it's more like a death sentence.

I find this attitude a little baffling. I have a friend who has an amazing body, primarily because all he eats is salad and tuna. He often longs to give in and have an ice cream sundae or pizza dripping with cheese, but he never does it. When I asked him once why he won't indulge, even a tiny bit, he said, "I'd rather have perfect abs than enjoy a few seconds of pleasure and have to work it off later."

This same friend finds it impossible to remain faithful to a lover. No sooner has he found a man he says he loves than he's off tricking with someone else. He sees no irony in this. In fact, he once asked me, "How can you have sex with the same guy over and over? Don't you ever want to try something different?"

"I'd rather know that my lover and I share something special than enjoy a few seconds of pleasure that I'll regret later," I said, remembering his answer to me.

He didn't get it. In his mind, giving up foods he might enjoy and even crave in exchange for a good body is worth it. But he's not willing to trade the momentary pleasure he gets when he has sex with someone other than his lover for a stronger, more committed relationship. At the same time, he wonders why his relationships never last more than six months.

Now, I'm not foolish enough to believe that monogamy is for everyone. I'm not even suggesting that it's for a lot of people. But I do think it gets a bad rap in the queer community, especially among gay men, and I'm a little tired of that. Over and over I've heard people talk about how liberating nonmonogamy is and how stifling and antiquated the notion of fidelity is.

Perhaps monogamy is old-fashioned. Maybe that's why I like it. I like the idea of growing old with one man and knowing that he's the only one for me in every way. I think there's something really special about agreeing to reserve intimacy for a partner, something that's diminished when those intimacies are shared with others. I like seeing my boyfriend across a room filled with people and knowing that if I walk up and slip my hand into his, he'll hold it, and that he wouldn't do that for anyone else.

I've been told by various people concerned for my well-being that my feelings about this are based on insecurities. I've been told I don't know the difference between sex and love. I've been told that I've bought into the heterosexual fallacy. And I've been told that I'll change my mind after a few years of married life.

Maybe I will. After all, as I said, I've been thinking about cheating on my boyfriend. Really, it's not that hard, is it? Sexual arousal is an easy trick to master, and it's not difficult to imagine myself in bed with, say, Ricky Martin or any of the Boston Bruins. In fact, it can be a lot of fun to think about such things.

But Ricky, hot as he is, fades from memory as soon as I've gotten off. And I'm betting the Bruins make better fantasy material than husbands. So I can say pretty much for certain that I'll stick with the man I've got. The truth is, there are generally a lot of guys who will have sex with you, but finding one who wants to hold your hand is worth a whole lot more.

So You Want to Be a Slut

People think it's easy being a slut. This is not true. It takes a great deal of effort and commitment, not to mention long hours in bars, men's rooms, and alleys. Being a slut is like being a sexual adventurer, going where others fear to tread and returning with descriptions of a way of life your less intrepid friends only wish they could experience for themselves. A slut is nothing less than a sexual ambassador who gives and gives and gives, thinking only of others. It is a profession to be honored, not ridiculed.

OK, perhaps not. But it *is* pretty difficult to maintain sluttiness on a consistent basis. Although many try, only a few attain this in their lifetimes. Those who do should take pride in their achievements, particularly as the only other choice is to feel like trash, and who needs that?

Are you one of the few, the proud, the slutty? Find out now.

1. How long do you wait to sleep with a guy you're interested in?
   (a) One date
   (b) Three dates
   (c) As long as it takes to get a cab to his place

2. When purchasing lube you buy it in:

   (a) Travel size

   (b) Economy size

   (c) Bulk

3. The worst part about public toilets is:
   (a) The smell
   (b) The rough toilet paper
   (c) The way the grout on the floor scratches up your knees

4. When walking through wooded areas you keep an eye out for:
   (a) Snakes
   (b) Birds
   (c) Guys waiting in the bushes

5. When someone on the street asks if you have the time, you:
   (a) Check your watch
   (b) Point them to the nearest clock
   (c) Say, "How long is it going to take?"

6. You can count the number of men you've slept with on:
   (a) One hand
   (b) Two hands
   (c) An abacus

7. If you had a Native American name to describe your sexual behavior, it would be:
   (a) Dances With Hand
   (b) Once in Blue Moon

(c) Feet to Heaven

8. Your exes refer to you in conversation as:
   (a) The one who never washed the dishes
   (b) The one who made me laugh
   (c) The one who I caught in bed with the softball team

9. Your idea of a committed relationship is one in which:
   (a) You have joint checking
   (b) You have a mortgage
   (c) You have a "don't ask, don't tell" policy

10. When entertaining company, you prefer them to sit:
    (a) On the couch
    (b) On the porch
    (c) On your face

ANSWERS:

1. (c)
2. (c)
3. (c)
4. (c)
5. (c)
6. (c)
7. (c)
8. (c)
9. (c)
10. (c)

SCORING:

Give yourself five points for each correct answer.

01–10: You aren't very good at this whoring around thing. In fact, you might want to try a little harder. You should be getting *some* sex every now and then.

15–20: You're not really a bad boy, but from time to time you've found yourself in bed with men who were strangers an hour before. Not that we haven't all done that, mind you, so don't feel bad.

25–30: You might not know this, but your friends take bets on who you'll go home with when you all go out. That good-boy facade isn't fooling anyone. We have the video footage of you in the Macy's men's room to prove it.

35–40: You're trampy and proud of it. While some of your friends find your behavior appalling, it's *your* stories they want to hear at brunch on Sunday.

45–50: It's people like you who made Sodom and Gomorrah—not to mention New York and San Francisco—such interesting places to live.

A friend of mine called today asking for advice. He was meeting some former coworkers for dinner, and he was bringing along his new boyfriend. Never having come out to his old office mates, he wasn't sure how to handle the situation. He wanted to know what *I* would do.

I told him to walk in, make sure all eyes were on him and his beloved, and say, "Everyone, this is Scott. He has the biggest dick you've ever seen, and I can get the whole thing down my throat."

Perhaps this seems a little shocking, even hostile. But it's certainly more fun than trying to figure out what to call a lover when introducing him to other people, especially people who don't know you're queer.

This is, I know, an age-old problem. Most of us have, at one time or another, had to wrestle with how to refer to our other halves. "Lover" is very romantic, like something out of a racy French novel. But for me it also conjures up an image of some 1970s disco reject with too many gold chains and a swinging bachelor pad he's anxious to show me. "Partner" suggests a law firm and business arrangements or maybe ballroom dancing. And while "boyfriend" is kind of cheery and devil-may-care, it lacks permanency, as if the relationship may or may not be all that serious.

Within our community, we understand this difficulty and cut each other some slack. If I'm talking to other gay people and mention that Patrick is my partner, they know what I mean. They also know that if I toss out a reference to "that guy I slept with last night," I mean him as well. Or at least I better mean him if I know what's good for me.

The problem is with the outside world. When dealing with straight people, what you call the object of your affection takes on great importance. I remember, years ago, being at a family function with my uncle David and his lover, George. My mother was introducing them to someone else, and she said, "This is my stepbrother, David, and this is his…" There was an awkward pause as she searched for a word to use. I could see David and George waiting expectantly to hear what would come next. Finally, my mother said, "His friend."

Well, yes, George was David's friend. They'd lived together for many years. They owned a house and a dog together. They wore wedding bands. They were definitely friends. But hearing them introduced that way reduced their relationship to the barest minimum. Perhaps the man they were being introduced to understood my mother's code word, but the implication was that what David and George represented was something we didn't talk about openly. And if he didn't understand what my mother meant by "friend," then David and George were invisible to him as gay people, which was even worse.

Straight people have it pretty easy when it comes to the whole name-calling issue. For them there's a definite progression in romantic relationships. A straight woman starts out with a boyfriend, moves on to a fiancé, and ends up with a husband. If she introduces the man she's brought to her friend's wedding as her "friend," we can generally infer that she's not dating anyone and this guy owes her a favor. Similarly, a straight woman's "lover" is most likely the guy she's sleeping with who isn't her husband. And any "partners" she has are likely just that. It's all very cut-and-dried.

This would never work with gay men. If, at a party, I'm introduced to a man and his "friend," I don't know if they just go rock climbing together or if they share a condo and bodily fluids. Likewise, someone's "partner" may in fact be his romantic other half, or he might simply do the accounting for their jointly owned design firm and be available for sleeping with, that is, if I didn't already have a "partner" of my own. You can see the problem. In the queer world, a man can have a friend, a boyfriend, a lover, and a partner, and they could all be the same person or they could all be different people.

When referring to Patrick in mixed company, I usually just say "Patrick," as in "Patrick and I are going to Palm Springs this weekend" or "I can't believe the stupid thing Patrick did last night." The people who know who he is understand. Those who don't will either make a logical assumption or ask, "Who's Patrick?" At which point I will tell them, randomly choosing from among the terms "boyfriend," "lover," "partner," and "stud beast."

I don't like having to do this. I don't like not having an adequate word to describe my relationship. It makes me feel as if no one has ever bothered to come up with one because they don't think there's any point. Straight people can call one another "husband" and "wife" and we know that there's a particular type of commitment between them. But queer people are denied that linguistic right. And when we do defiantly call our lovers our husbands or wives, it unfortunately just sounds like we're trying too hard.

Recently I was at a store looking at dishes that Patrick's daughter—who is getting married later this year—had put on her want list. I had Patrick on the cell phone, and we were discussing the situation. The sales clerk who was helping me stood, listening, as we talked for probably 10 minutes, during which time the words "honey," "sweetie," and "I love you" were uttered. When I hung up I turned to her and said, "OK, we'll take them."

As the young woman was ringing up the order she said, "It's really nice of you to get these for her," meaning, of course, Patrick's daughter.

"You know how it is," I replied. "Fathers can never say no to their daughters."

The woman smiled. "He must be a great dad," she said, beaming. "And you must be the best brother ever."

I looked at her for a moment, trying to decide what to say next. Beside her a male clerk—who was clearly gay and who had helped Patrick and me on several previous occasions—was trying not to laugh.

"I'm not her brother," I said. "I'm the boyfriend."

The young woman's smile turned to a look of confusion. She studied me for a minute, then said, "But what about her fiancé?"

This time the male clerk did laugh, and so did I. "I'm the *father's* boyfriend," I clarified as the girl looked at us blankly.

The young woman blushed deeply. "Oh, God," she

said. "I'm so sorry. I didn't think... I mean... Well, you don't *look* gay. I just assumed that..."

She stopped talking, her face red as she fumbled for something to say that wouldn't get her any deeper into the hole she'd already dug. "Well, you must be the best *boyfriend* ever," she said finally.

"I like to think so," I answered. "But I'm not exactly objective on that point."

Now, of course, this was funny. When I told Patrick—and anyone else who would listen—about it, we all had a good laugh. But it also points out just how unused people are to perceiving two men as being a couple. This young woman heard me call Patrick "honey." She heard us having the kind of discussion that couples generally have. But something in her mind prevented her from seeing us for what we are.

Several years after the party where my uncle David and his lover were introduced as "friends," they were both killed in a car accident. They were buried in cemeteries thousands of miles apart, George with his family and David with his. It was as if they'd never been together, never shared a life, a home, a dog, a bed. People looking at their gravestones would never know that either had loved another man, had been part of a relationship filled with love and trust and hope. No one would know that they had not only lived together but died together. Once again, what they were to one another had been obscured.

Then, recently, my mother called to tell me that David's sister had placed a headstone for George next to the one for David, along with some of George's ashes. I hope people walking through that cemetery stop and look at those headstones. I hope they notice the different last names and the same date of death. And more than anything, I hope they understand that the two men buried there were much more than friends.

MY WORLD

Imagine, if you will, a world without electricity. Or airplanes. Or Hollywood. Think about what kind of world that would be.

What it would be is the world that would exist if things had been left up to me. Not that I don't like electricity or airplanes or Hollywood (well, I'm not wild about Hollywood). It's just that, frankly, I would never have gotten around to inventing them. It would have taken far too much effort.

From time to time—generally while I'm supposed to be writing a book—I spend long hours simply looking around at all of the things that exist despite the best efforts of people like myself. It's overwhelming, really, to know that had I been running things we probably wouldn't now be enjoying such wondrous creations as Hello Kitty, blue cheese, and public education. In fact, we would probably all be sitting around naked in fairly damp caves gnawing on sticks.

This is disconcerting. I like to think that I am at least marginally intelligent. I like to think that, if stranded in the wilderness, I could last perhaps 10 minutes or so before succumbing to heatstroke, lack of water, or hyenas. And perhaps I could. But I know with absolute certainty that had the development of the civilized world been in my hands, our entire planet would currently look like an Alabama trailer park just after a tornado has passed through: lots of piles of formless refuse and crowds of bewildered people staring up at the sky.

Had I been running things, we wouldn't know there *was* China, let alone be enjoying take-out sweet-and-sour chicken. Not for us would be the joys of cello suites, gin rummy, and the flush toilet. In all likelihood we'd be standing at the edge of the ocean, waiting for something to happen.

Last year I went to India with my friend Katherine to look at temples (OK, to get away from my editors). One morning we were standing in the middle of a particularly beautiful temple, looking all around us at the intricately carved statues and decorations. Each stone of the temple walls fit perfectly against the next. The archways between the rooms were marvels of engineering. The temple rose hundreds of feet into the air, each level more exquisite that the last. It was, in short, breathtaking.

As we stood there, gazing at the statue whose shrine it was, Katherine turned to me. "You realize that they did all this using basically their hands and some little bits of metal, right?"

I knew exactly what she was getting at. Only an hour before, she and I had been totally unable to remove the childproof top from the bottle of malaria pills we were supposed to be taking. But hundreds of years earlier, some enterprising people had built *an entire temple* without the aid of machinery, computerized drafting programs, or chilled drinks. It was demoralizing.

Perhaps I'm not being fair. Maybe our ancestors built and discovered and set forth to conquer because there was nothing else to do. Nowadays we have responsibilities to keep us at home, not to mention air conditioning, frozen pizza, and Sony PlayStations. It isn't our fault that Lewis and Clark, Thomas Edison, and all the rest of them beat us to the punch, is it? After all, they weren't really doing anything else. I'm sure that they too would be hard-pressed to wander around in the wilderness or spend hours in a lab trying to make a lightbulb if they knew that they could just as easily be trying to reach level 17 on Crash Bandicoot.

Or perhaps not. Perhaps the drive to invent and build has simply been bred out of us. Still, it's astonishing to think of how bleak things would be if people like myself had had our way. Take pretty much anything from modern culture, and you can safely assume that it would never have gotten any help from me in its creation. Railroads? Never. We'd still be plodding along dirt tracks, taking six months to get from our huts in New York to those all-important pitch meetings in L.A. If New York and L.A. even existed, which I sincerely doubt.

Or what about this computer that I'm typing on? Forget it. I can barely understand what it does; the very idea that someone *invented* it is utterly unbelievable. Someone once tried to explain to me how hitting the L key on my keyboard is translated into a string of 1s and 0s that the computer does something with. I do not believe this. I do not understand how it is possible. This is a pile of plastic and metal with some electricity running through it. As far as I'm concerned, there are little people inside busily writing down everything I type, like that bird on Fred Flintstone's typewriter. I have proof of this:

Sometimes I leave food out for them, and it's always gone in the morning.

It's not that I can't grasp the concept of *wanting* to invent things. I can, for example, fully appreciate that somewhere along the line someone looked at a tree and thought, "This would make nice lumber." That's where my interest in the subject stops, however. I cannot even begin to comprehend having the wherewithal to get from that fleeting thought to making a saw and actually turning the tree *into* lumber. This is way beyond me. As for turning the lumber into anything else, forget it.

Of course, there are other things that I'm very proud *not* to have had a hand in. I hardly think, for example, that claiming responsibility for things like the Inquisition, textured ceilings, or electronic dance music is something to put on your résumé. But I can't help but feel slightly jealous of the people who came up with these things. At least they *made* something. I do not make things. I buy things. I like places like Banana Republic and Ikea and Ralphs because they do all the work for me. (Well, really, I suspect that underpaid children in Taiwan do all the work for me, but I don't like to think about that.) I am happy to pay them for doing this, because I know that without them I'd be sitting in a tree somewhere scratching myself and waiting for the fruit to ripen.

During all of the fuss about the turn of the millennium, when people were stockpiling food and building bunkers and whatnot, I did nothing. I knew there was no point. If the world as we know it was going to come to an end, I was going to go with it. Sure, I might have been able to buy up lots of cans of SpaghettiOs and lay in a supply of bottled water. But what would happen when those ran out? I'd be dead meat. And really, I probably wouldn't have lasted even as long as the SpaghettiOs. As soon as I wasn't able to check my E-mail 16 times a day, what would be the point of living?

Some people aspire to be the first one living on Mars or to invent the next microprocessor. I aspire to be Amish. There was a large Amish community near where I grew up, and it was always a treat for me to visit them when my mother went to buy eggs or quilts, which happened once or twice a year. "Don't stare," she'd warn as we drove up the long dusty road to their cluster of houses. "Remember, they're different."

Yes, they were different. And yes, I stared. But not because I thought they were weird. It was because secretly I wanted to live with them. I knew *they* would understand the comfort I found in a way of life that didn't require me to know anything more complicated than how to light a candle or stick a seed in the ground (and I was even doubtful about my ability to do these things). Free of electricity and cars and telephones, they existed in a simpler place, one where no one expected anything of anyone. (I sincerely doubt that any Amish person has ever called up a writer demanding to know where his manuscript is.) What a relief it would be, I thought, to be among such people.

Now it's too late. I'm far too used to my cable television and my PalmPilot and the Internet. Although I will never understand how they came to be or how they work, I am happy to ride on trains and use my credit cards and stick contact lenses in my eyes every morning. And I am thankful for the people who did invent these things, because without them I would be nothing. I just hope they don't expect anything in return.

The Gay Celebrity

The gay celebrity—like the male nurse and the child actor—is an unusual creature. Its very name speaks volumes: The gay celebrity is celebrated not so much for its achievements per se but for the fact that it has achieved them *while being gay.* This is the key. And an important key it is. Because nine times out of 10, no one would care about the gay celebrity if not for the gayness to which it is attached.

This is not to say that the gay celebrity is not talented. Not at all. It's simply to say that this talent, removed from the celebrity's gayness, might not be as remarked upon. The whole gay thing makes the celebrity slightly more interesting, more worthy of attention. It is, in short, that upon which it trades.

The origins of the gay celebrity are found in the mid-to-late 1980s, a time when being gay was decidedly cool. This period saw an explosion in gay-themed magazines, the rise of "lesbian chic," and an increase in disposable income. At the same time, a number of semifamous people found their careers waning and a number of wanting-to-be-famous newcomers were looking for ways to jump-start their careers. Magazine editors, looking for people to put on their covers to sell the new gay magazines, were not slow in noticing this. Thus was born the gay celebrity. This new phenomenon quickly established itself, with the following categories emerging.

GAY ACTORS

There have always been gay actors, but until the advent of the gay celebrity they were our "little secret." We all knew that Rock Hudson was a Mary, and Monty Clift couldn't pull the wool over the eyes of those of us who knew him as "Princess Tiny Meat." But the Gay Actor today is something different. He is a darling *because* he is gay. Generally he has appeared in only one or two things—perhaps an art film or a sitcom. Often he has seen a successful career come to an end and is looking for a way back. We don't care. He's gay! It used to be that actors needing press simply checked into rehab. Now they come out.

Good Examples: Ellen, Harvey Fierstein
Bad Examples: Anne Heche, Porn stars in one-man shows

GAY ATHLETES

The idea of professional baseball players, hockey players, or football players coming out is very exciting indeed. The reality of gay sportsmen, unfortunately, has been somewhat less thrilling. (Gay figure skaters? There's a huge shock.) Still, we love our gay sports figures. They are, after all, jocks, and that's something. But apart from the notable exceptions of women tennis players and Greg Louganis, few of our gay sports celebrities have achieved all that much. And cute as he is, how many of you had ever heard of Billy Bean before he came out? I thought so.

Good Examples: Martina Navratilova, Amélie Mauresmo
Bad Examples: Women golfers

GAY MUSICIANS

The queer community had its own excellent musicians long before anyone started taking notice. (Hello? Cris Williamson, anyone?) But when Melissa Etheridge announced to the world that she was a dyke, everyone started doing it. Suddenly we were supposed to buy some band's CD just because the bass player happened to be a fag or flock to a performer's shows because once, when she was 14, she kissed another girl. "That's one more for our side!" we'd cheer, ignoring the fact that the singer in question didn't come out until he was arrested for having sex in a public toilet. Who cares? He's gay! It used to be that musicians had to actually make good music to get noticed. Now all it takes is writing cryptic lyrics using same-sex pronouns.

Good Examples: k.d. lang, Elton John
Bad Examples: Rob Halford, Michael Stipe

GAY ACTIVISTS

Nowhere can so many with so little to say become so famous as in the queer community. All it takes is attitude and the firm belief that you have been picked on unfairly. Combine that with a petulant tone of voice and the ability to look presentable while talking on CNN and you're all set. You receive extra bonus points if you have achieved your celebrity simply for being related to someone in politics, having once been part of the "ex-gay" movement, or getting kicked out of a scouting organization.

Good Examples: Urvashi Vaid, Andrew Sullivan
Bad Examples: Candace Gingrich, Andrew Sullivan

GAY CHILDREN OF FAMOUS PEOPLE

There's no purer form of celebrity than being famous for absolutely no reason other than having had famous parents. Celebrity is a hereditary condition, and if you can imply that perhaps homosexuality is as well (Headline: "Hollywood Causes Gayness"), you're sure to be quoted extensively. Besides, magazine editors know that if they're nice to you, your mommy and daddy might agree to appear on future covers.

Good Examples: None
Bad Examples: Chastity Bono, Jason Gould, Christopher Rice

NONGAY GAY CELEBRITIES

This special category is reserved for gay icons—those people we wish so much *were* gay that we've turned them into honorary gay celebrities. Their fame flows directly from us, their queer fans. We keep them alive long after the nongay world would have left them lying on the side of the road, gasping for a sip of mineral water and a ticket to the Oscars. We are their reason for living, the reason they keep smiling. In return, they allow us to feel that they are *ours,* and this is a very special thing indeed. The

Nongay Gay Celebrity is distinguished by its ability to launch a "comeback" with each new album, its eagerness to thank its gay fans in interviews, and its repeated appearance on the cover of *The Advocate*—even though there are many more interesting and newsworthy stories to be covered in any given week.

Good Examples: Madonna, Cher, Bette Midler
Bad Examples: None

CALIFORNIA BEAMING

I have become a bad person, one of those people I used to hate. This realization came to me this afternoon as I was walking the dog and, while he was peeing, I decided to call someone on my cell phone. There Roger was, happily lifting his leg on a palm tree, and I was talking on a cell phone. But that is not the worst part. No, the absolute worst part, the part that makes this situation completely intolerable, is that I was wearing sunglasses.

I blame all of this on California. When I announced to my friends that I was moving to Los Angeles, they were not happy. My friend Gretchen in particular was quite displeased. Gretchen grew up in San Francisco, and has the same marked distaste for Southern California that those who live in New England have for, well, pretty much the entire rest of the country. As far as she was concerned, in leaving Boston for L.A. I was leaving civilization and heading for a barren wasteland peopled by savages and monsters.

"You'd better not turn into one of those horrible people who *do* lunch," she said meaningfully.

"Please," I said. "I don't even *do* dishes."

But I think I might really be becoming one of those people. As evidence I present the aforementioned cell phone and sunglasses. Yes, I know, people all over the place have cell phones and sunglasses, even in Bangladesh and Namibia. But here in Southern California they're more than just mere cell phones and sunglasses. They are accessories. You're not allowed to leave the house without them. And I don't.

That's not all. I'm embarrassed to tell you the rest, lest you think terrible things about me. But yes, it's true. In addition to the cell phone and the sunglasses there's—oh, how can I say it—the PalmPilot.

There. The worst of it is out on the table for you to see in all of its ugliness, all of its naked, brazen awfulness. For the truth is, I have become a sunglasses-wearing, cell phone–using, PalmPilot-checking nightmare.

I don't know how this happened. I mean, I know how it happened, I bought the cell phone and the sunglasses and the PalmPilot. But when did I become a person who wanted such things? In my defense, I really did *need* them at the time. The cell phone, for example. I got it when I was on my last book tour. How else was I supposed to remain in contact with my agents, the dog sitter, and the television producer who was going to make me famous with my own television show. Oh, dear, now that I'm actually putting it all into words it doesn't sound quite so innocent after all.

Well, the PalmPilot then. I got *that* because I needed something to keep my addresses in. And my schedule. And besides, you can point it at other PalmPilots and beam information around like the Star Wars missile defense system shooting lasers hither and yon. Surely that alone was justification enough for its purchase.

Or perhaps not. I'm starting to sense a disturbing trend here. But surely you can't fault me on the sunglasses. I'd never owned a pair before I moved to California. Even then I was determined not to become one of those people who peer out at the world from behind tinted lenses. But this *sun*! You can't even imagine. The sun in Boston was a pale, dreary little thing hiding its sleepy face in the clouds. Here in Southern California it's a great glowing ball that hovers only inches above our heads, toasting us like burgers beneath a heat lamp at Carl's Jr. My first week here I went about squinting at everything, feeling, I imagine, much like those shepherds to whom the Angel of the Lord unexpectedly appeared in the Bible. Every time I stepped outdoors I kept expecting to hear loud voices shouting, "Lo! And unto you is given delicious Chinese takeout and lovely beaches!"

So that's how the sunglasses happened. And really, I don't think they're such a bad thing. It's just that added to the cell phone and the PalmPilot, it's slightly too much.

But I can't get rid of them, especially now that I live in Southern California. It's like they're requirements or something, the same way you're expected to wear flannel if you live in Seattle or be rude if you live in New York. (I lived in New York for a decade, so I know of what I speak. Don't send letters.) Having lived for more than 30 years on the East Coast, I didn't really know what to expect when I moved to California. I have friends who tried to do it before I did, and they all rushed back after less than a month. "You can't believe how shallow they are out there!" they cried. "There's no *culture.*"

This is not true. There *is* culture in Southern California. True, it's less about, say, going to the symphony and more about going to the mall. But it's culture nonetheless. And, frankly, I like it. I always fell asleep at the symphony anyway. Here I go to baseball games and

Disneyland, which is much more my speed. On the East Coast I always felt pressured to think nice thoughts about art and opera and theater. Now I can be my beer-drinking, Bruce Willis movie–watching, pickup-driving self and no one bats an eye. Culture be damned. I have Koo Koo Roo and Angelyne to keep me happy.

Besides, I moved here, at least in part, to be involved in the television industry. Never mind that since arriving the most involved I've been with TV is to turn mine on so I can watch *Buffy the Vampire Slayer*. That's not the point. The point is that I am *connected*. My cell phone and PalmPilot help me stay *in the loop*. (The sunglasses, in case you're wondering, just look cool.) At any given moment I'm ready for a producer to call me on my cell phone and say, "Can you take a meeting this Friday?" At which point I'll fire up my PalmPilot, check my calendar, and say cool-ly, "I think I can fit you in between my pitch at DreamWorks and my dinner with Paramount."

Granted, this scenario is realized far less often than one would hope. But it *could* happen. It *will* happen. (Visualization is something else they make you do here in California.) And when it does, I'll be very happy that I have these things, even if they do make me a horrible person that my friend Gretchen is ashamed to know. In the mean-time, the cell phone makes it much easier to call my boyfriend from the produce section at Ralphs to ask, "Asparagus or broccoli?" And if you happen to see me walking around with my PalmPilot out, beam me your info. I'll call you. We'll do lunch.

So You Want to Be a Gym Rat

It's no secret that a lot of gay men are obsessed with their bodies. More than most people, we spend a great deal of time worrying about how we look, particularly about how we look naked. Gyms are filled with queers pumping up, and the gay gym rat is a peculiar breed with its own culture and habits. Not every guy who picks up a weight or steps on a treadmill can call himself a true gym rat. To attain that status requires a little something more. Do you have what it takes to be one? Answer the following questions and find out.

1. The optimum time for going to the gym is:
   (a) When the hottest guys are there
   (b) When it's least crowded and you won't have to wait
   (c) Saturday afternoon so you look pumped up for
       Saturday night

2. The best source of protein in a workout diet is found in:
   (a) Chicken
   (b) Sara Lee Pound Cake
   (c) The sauna

3. When working out, the term "spotting" refers to:
   (a) The stains you get in your shorts from thinking
       about the cute guy riding the exercise bike in front
       of yours
   (b) Noticing the hot number with great biceps who

you saw weeks before and have been hoping to run into again

(c) Helping out a buddy by encouraging him during a set and being ready to grab the weights should he falter on that final rep

4. The most appropriate clothing to wear while working out is:
   (a) Something that absorbs sweat
   (b) Something that shows off your ass
   (c) A snowsuit

5. The most appropriate use of the communal showers is for:
   (a) Comparing dick size
   (b) Comparing muscle size
   (c) Comparing shampoos

6. The most important feature when choosing a personal trainer is:
   (a) How cute he is
   (b) How much he charges
   (c) How long it will take him to pack 25 pounds of muscle on you

7. After a good hard workout you feel:
   (a) Ready to throw up
   (b) Ready for anything
   (c) Ready for a nap

8. You think Bill Phillips is:
   (a) God

(b) Satan

(c) Who?

9. Creatine is:

(a) The period between the Jurassic and the Paleolithic

(b) A supplement that prevents muscle fatigue

(c) A miracle fabric that looks just like silk but is machine washable

10. Complete the phrase "No pain, no _____ ."

(a) Gain

(b) Cookie

(c) Chiropractor

ANSWERS:

1. (b)
2. (a)
3. (c)
4. (a)
5. (b)
6. (c)
7. (b)
8. (a)
9. (b)
10. (a)

SCORING:

Give yourself five points for each correct answer.

01–10: Lazy bastard. The only reason you would go to the gym is if they were giving away free doughnuts. But good for you. All that time you're not spending lifting weights means you can watch more TV!

15–20: Every so often you go to the gym, but probably you stop after a day or two when you realize that those weights are heavier than they look.

25–30: You get yourself into the gym fairly often, but sometimes when you're lifting you find yourself thinking, *I could be eating pizza right now,* and you hit the showers.

35–40: You like to keep in shape, so you go to the gym a couple of times a week. But I bet your favorite activity is hanging around the locker room waiting for guys to change.

45–50: You're such a rat you might as well have a tail. You're the kind of guy the rest of us stare at while we're struggling to do another rep on the bench press. We all hope that you have a *really* small dick.

The Final Chapter

In the past year, two of my favorite queer bookstores—Boston's wonderful Glad Day Book Shop and New York's A Different Light—closed their doors. The story of the independent bookstore being forced out of business by the ever-encroaching chains, online stores, and rising operating costs isn't a new one. When it comes to queer, alternative, or women's bookstores, however, the casualties have been particularly high.

The difficulty queer bookstores are having staying open is disturbing. But this is more than just a business issue.

I walked into my first gay bookstore a dozen years ago, when I moved to New York and discovered A Different Light, then located on Hudson Street. The store was a funky mix of books, magazines, T-shirts, posters, and various other items devoted to queer culture. For me, newly released from a religious college and starving for anything gay, it was like walking into a candy store. I bought more books than I could read, just to have them on the shelves. I found out about ACT UP and Queer Nation meetings by reading the fliers pinned to the jumbled mess that was the community bulletin board. I met my first boyfriend there.

Similarly, Boston's Glad Day Book Shop was one of the first places I went after I moved to Boston in the winter of 1995. The store looked a lot like the old A Different Light, which I loved, and the manager, the wonderful John Mitzel, was always up for a half hour of book talk and good old fashioned gossip. The store closed shortly before I left Boston for California, and I remember thinking, when I heard it was shutting its doors, that now I had one less reason to stay and face another frigid Beantown winter.

As someone who makes a living by writing, I understand all too well the fragile financial web of buying and selling books. I know that small stores simply can't offer the same discounts, variety, and instant gratification that chains can. And yes, I've bought books online when I couldn't find them at my local independent store or when I just haven't felt like leaving the house. Besides, my own books sell very well through those same outlets, so I can't complain too much. Especially when I know there are lots of people out there buying queer books online who would never buy them if they had to walk into a store.

But I think we need to look at what we're losing every time a queer bookstore closes. This isn't just about books, although we need to keep in mind that long before the chain stores made those little sections for "gay literature," small independent bookstores made queer literature available by hunting down everything that was in print, and long before mainstream publishers took any interest in gay books, there were small queer publishers putting them out at great trouble and expense.

But, as I said, this isn't just about the books. You can get gay books pretty much anywhere these days. The disappearance of the queer bookstore is frightening for a larger reason. It used to be that these stores functioned as de facto community centers, information libraries, and even pickup joints. Going into one, you felt that you belonged there. These were *your* books and *your* people and *your* space. Browsing through the latest issue of *Out* or reading the first chapter of the new Andrew Holleran or Dorothy Allison to see if it hooks you just isn't the same when you do it at Giant Colossal Super Bookstore surrounded by 6 billion copies of the 15th Harry Potter installment, Oprah's latest pick, and a stack of Dr. Laura's current abomination.

Last summer I flew to Chicago for the annual Lambda Literary Awards, where my book *That's Mr. Faggot to You* received a Lammy for best humor book. On the way home the next morning, when I sent my carry-on through the security scanner, I was asked to step aside and open my bag for inspection. Having gone through exactly the same thing the previous year, I knew what they were looking for.

"It's an award," I said as I took out the Lammy nestled in the center of the suitcase and held it out for inspection.

The security guard doing the check took the award— a Lucite block with a medal embedded in the center—and stared at it.

"We thought it might be a bomb," she explained. Then she took a closer look. "Gay and lesbian book award?" she said, staring at me curiously. "They have an award for that?"

Yes, they have an award for that. And we have that award because we like to honor books by and about queer people and those people's lives. As more and more of gay culture is subsumed by the mainstream, it's easy to forget that our inclusion in that mainstream is largely dependent upon what they can get out of our culture. Our words stay in print as long as they make money, not necessarily as long as they're needed. Our voices are heard as long as what we say isn't too offensive.

So the next time you need to pick up a book, please consider taking a trip to your local queer store, if you have one. If you don't, please consider asking whatever store you go to to stock more queer titles. As for the booksellers out there, my heartfelt appreciation to all of you working within the chains to make sure (often covertly) that queer books don't disappear. And finally, to the great folks at Glad Day and A Different Light—and to everyone who runs a gay bookstore—a big thank-you for keeping us at least one step away from the jaws of assimilation.

Gay Like Me:
Being a Transcript of a Lost *Advocate*
Magazine Interview*

In the summer of 2001 the movie *One Night Stand* played to enthusiastic audiences in gay film festivals around the country. The film, directed by rising queer filmmaker Stephen Rowson-Craig, is a poignant coming-of-age story centered on the character of Jamie, a college freshman who, having escaped the confines of his small-town life and ultrareligious family, finds himself thrust into a world where he is free to make his own choices for the first time in his life. Jamie, who has been raised to think of homosexuality as a sin, is terrified when he wakes up the morning after going to his first frat party to find himself in bed—naked—with a hunky jock named Pete. At first neither guy is exactly sure what happened or how they ended up in bed together. But when one of Pete's frat brothers gleefully produces a videotape showing Jamie and Pete engaging in drunken sex, the two find themselves at the center of a controversy that will change both their lives forever.

The following is the transcript of an interview done with actor Draper Avery, who plays Jamie in the film. The interview was scheduled to run in *The Advocate* but never did. It appears here for the first time in print.

*NOTE: This is a *parody*, people. Don't go looking for this film. It doesn't exist.

The Advocate: Obviously you play a gay man in the movie. Are you gay?
Draper Avery: No.

TA: You answered very quickly and emphatically. Does it bother you that people might think you're gay because you played a gay character?
DA: Not at all. But you asked if I *was* gay, and I'm not.

TA: Do you always feel like you have to be defensive about that?
DA: No. I don't think I'm defensive about it.

TA: Has anyone ever thought you were gay?
DA: Not that I know of.

TA: Why not?
DA: Excuse me?

TA: Why not? Don't you think it's possible that someone might think you're gay?
DA: I guess they could. But no one ever has.

TA: That you know of. But maybe they're just not telling you. Does it bother you if people think you're gay and don't say anything?
DA: No.

TA: Have you ever thought about being gay?
DA: I've never considered becoming gay, if that's what you mean. But I've thought about what it must be like. I mean, I had to for the film.

TA: And what do you think it must be like being gay?
DA: Not much different from being straight, really.

TA: Except the part where we're discriminated against every second of our lives because we're gay. Did you ever think about that?
DA: Well, yes. That's kind of what the film is about.

TA: But going through that experience in character never made you think you might be gay?
DA: Never.

TA: Did anyone who worked on the film think you might be gay?
DA: If they did, they didn't say anything to me. Plus, my wife was on the set a lot, so I think people figured it out pretty quickly.

TA: Did you make her come to the set?
DA: No. She wanted to come.

TA: So you didn't make her come as a way of letting people know you're not gay.
DA: Not at all.

TA: Right. So how would you feel if you knew the person interviewing you was gay?
DA: I wouldn't mind. I mean, you're gay, right?

TA: Well, you should never assume such things about people, should you? After all, I could just as easily be straight.

DA: You're right. I'm sorry.

TA: It's OK. I *am* gay. I was just making a point. So how would you feel if you knew the person interviewing you was gay *and* won a Grammy.
DA: That's cool.

TA: Did it ever occur to you that gay people could win Grammys?
DA: I guess I never really thought about it.

TA: Don't you think that's a homophobic response? I mean, why shouldn't gay people win Grammys too?
DA: They should. I mean, a lot of gay people are musical.

TA: There you go, being homophobic again. Do you just assume that because people are gay that they like musicals?
DA: No. I was just trying to be funny.

TA: Oh. Let's move on. When did you first know you were straight?
DA: I don't think I ever really thought about it.

TA: Of course not. Straight people don't have to think about things like that, right? Only gay people do.
DA: Well, I mean, it's just who I am.

TA: What do you think it would be like if straight people had to come out to their families the way gay people do?
DA: I guess that would be weird.

TA: Weird? Why is coming out "weird"?

DA: Well, it would be weird having to say, "Mom. Dad. I have something to tell you. I'm straight." [*Laughs*]

TA: You think it's funny?

DA: Yeah, I do. Don't you?

TA: Hmm. So do you know Cher?

DA: Cher? No, I don't know her.

TA: Do you know anyone who knows Cher?

DA: I don't think so. Oh, wait, I remember the guy who did my makeup on the movie said something about having gone to Cher's house once.

TA: Was he gay?

DA: [*Shrugging*] I guess so. I mean he was a makeup... I don't know.

TA: What do you think it would be like to know Cher?

DA: I have no idea.

TA: You mean you can't even *imagine* being friends with Cher? Why is that so hard?

DA: I just don't know what it would be like is all. It's not like I would *mind* being friends with Cher.

TA: I see. That's very enlightened of you. Tell me, if you *were* gay, what kind of guy would you be interested in?

DA: I don't think I can answer that. I'm not attracted to men, so I don't really see what other people find attractive about them.

TA: You've never been attracted to a man?
DA: Never.

TA: Your kissing scenes in the movie are so realistic. Are you saying that's the first time you've kissed another man?
DA: The first time I've kissed one romantically, yes.

TA: Did you like it?
DA: It didn't do anything for me, if that's what you mean.

TA: So you weren't aroused?
DA: No. But it's very difficult to be aroused during a scene, whether it's with a man or with a woman. There are so many other people around, plus the lights and the boom and everything else. It's not exactly conducive to romance.

TA: But if those things weren't there—if you were just alone with another man—you don't think you would get aroused kissing him?
DA: I really doubt it.

TA: Your character has to come out to his best friend back home over Thanksgiving break. Did you like Thanksgiving when you were a kid?
DA: Sure. Who doesn't like Thanksgiving?

TA: Do you think that gay people enjoy Thanksgiving the same way straight people do?
DA: I think they probably do. Who doesn't love the Macy's parade, right?

TA: If you had to come out to your parents, would you do it at Thanksgiving?
DA: I don't think that would be the best time, no.

TA: If you *were* gay, when *would* you come out to your parents?
DA: Probably after my father had been drinking heavily.

TA: Has anyone ever come out to you?
DA: No.

TA: So you don't have any gay friends?
DA: I have gay friends. But none of them ever had to come out to me.

TA: How would you feel if one did?
DA: I wouldn't care. If the person is my friend, I don't care if he's gay or straight.

TA: What if one of your children came out to you?
DA: I like to think I'd be OK with it.

TA: But you don't know?
DA: I don't think you know until it happens.

TA: Do you know any gay people in Hollywood?
DA: Sure.

TA: Do you know if any of the following people are really gay: Tom Cruise, Melanie Mayron, Kevin Spacey, Jennifer Aniston, Paul Newman, Joanne Woodward, Brad Pitt, Mary-

Kate and/or Ashley Olsen, Bert and Ernie, or Tinky Winky?
DA: I don't know any of those people, so I can't say for sure.

TA: Do you *think* any of those people might be gay?
DA: Maybe.

TA: Why do you think they don't come out then?
DA: It's difficult to be out in Hollywood. People want to perceive you in certain ways, and if they know you're gay sometimes that's difficult.

TA: If you were gay, would you come out?
DA: Probably not.

TA: But then you could be on the cover of *The Advocate*.
DA: I'm going to be on the cover anyway, right?

TA: We'll see. We haven't heard back from Cher yet.

[*Sound of tape recorder clicking off.*]

Food for Thought

I have newfound sympathy for supermodels.

A couple of months ago I started a new workout program. The reasons for this are many, and I won't go into them here because they aren't really important to this particular story. The upshot is that I decided I wanted to put on 25 pounds. Yes, that's right, I voluntarily set about *gaining* weight.

Now, you might think that this is an easy thing to do, right? Most of us put on weight just *looking* at food. Gaining 25 pounds, then, should be as simple as eating everything in sight. But I wanted this to be *good* weight, the kind made of muscle, not fat. This kind of weight, as I soon discovered, is not so easy to add.

In addition to getting myself to the gym every day, this weight-gain plan involves a fairly strict, low-fat diet. I thought I was eating pretty well before. No dozen doughnuts for me. No piles of fried food or bowls of ice cream floating in chocolate sauce. But compared to how I eat now, I was clearly a gigantic hog, a human vacuum sucking up every spare bit of fat in the universe.

On this new diet, practically everything truly enjoyable to eat is forbidden. I'm allowed to have fish and chicken, all right, but I'm not allowed to smother it in cheese sauce or mushrooms sauteed in butter. I can eat potatoes, but no sour cream or butter may mar their virginal whiteness. Salt is frowned upon. Instead I eat mountains of broiled chicken breasts and tuna steak upon tuna steak. My refrigerator is crammed full of them, along with gallons and gallons of water. If I were to die and investigators opened the icebox looking for clues, they could not be blamed for thinking that I was either stockpiling for an imminent Arctic expedition or raising alligators.

I know this is a healthy way to eat. I remind myself of that as I'm chewing on my green beans and broiled red snapper. I repeat it like a mantra as I run on the treadmill, picturing a giant key lime pie hovering in front of me like the spaceship in *Close Encounters of the Third Kind.* "Healthy, healthy, healthy," I think, breathing in and out as the brown rice I had for lunch soars through my insides like a cleansing wave.

The thing that frightens me most about the diet isn't the food, but how compulsive I've become about it. Before, I would open the peanut butter and eat it right out of the jar without a care. Now I study the label and recoil at the many grams of fat in each tablespoon. I picture myself eating it and the horrid fat immediately taking up residence in my waist, where it will steadfastly refuse to budge no matter how many sit-ups I do.

Because every pound of fat lost and muscle gained seems to require monumental amounts of willpower and working out, I've become reluctant to do anything to counter the effects of the program. Several times I've found myself staring at a coffee cake my boyfriend has left on the counter or gazing longingly at the pizza he's brought home. Part of me wants to just dig in. But another part, the part that loves the fact that I've gone from a 35 waist to a 32, won't let me. The other day I actually spent a good hour wondering if I could put an M&M in my mouth for a minute and then spit it out without ruining utterly the accumulated results of my diet.

In the past, I ate whenever I wanted to. If I felt like having a handful of potato chips while I was writing, I did. If I wanted to chow down on a carton of chicken and black bean sauce from the local Chinese restaurant at midnight, I just picked up the phone and ordered. But now I eat six times a day, at very specific intervals. Because of this I find myself waiting expectantly for each feeding time to come. I understand now why the dog gets so excited when 3 o'clock rolls around. Sometimes I'll be working and suddenly an alarm will go off in my head, as if a little man is madly screaming, "Mid-morning snack!" or "Dinner!"

The really weird thing is that no one is preventing me from eating other things. It's all voluntary. But whenever I find myself tempted to cheat, I don't do it. The allure of finally having washboard abs is that strong, and I'm not going to let a carton of Ben & Jerry's stand in my way. On days when I *really* feel like giving in and consuming an entire box of Cap'n Crunch, I weight myself repeatedly and remind myself that I'm almost halfway to my goal.

I like to think that if I were *really* suffering under this diet, I would quit. But I don't know that I would. There's something magical about watching your body change, something enchanting about realizing that you can alter the size and shape of the costume you walk around in every day of your life. While this can be empowering, it also scares me a little, especially when I think about what it all means. I realized the other day that most of my gay male friends are on some kind of diet. Most also work out a couple of times a week. When I look at these men, I think they look fine just the way they are. But they all have something they want to change—a waistline that isn't small enough, a chest that isn't large enough, arms that could fill out a T-shirt just the tiniest bit more firmly. No one is ever quite satisfied.

I'll be the first to say that many gay men suffer from severe vanity. But I'm beginning to wonder when body consciousness crosses the line into obsessiveness. Is the fact that more and more of my friends are talking seriously about liposuction and face-lifts simply a sign that we're more willing to consider changes we never thought about before, or are we simply succumbing to the myth that physical beauty equals self-worth?

Just a few years ago, I thought men who spent a lot of time in the gym were crazy. Now I find myself doing it along with them. In the locker room I look at guys with bodies I admire and wonder if they go home and think about eating entire boxes of cookies while they have a can of tuna for lunch. Later, as I stand in my kitchen watching the blender whip up one of the three protein shakes I drink every day, I remember when I used to guzzle whole milk and think nothing of it. Now drinking anything stronger than water makes me worry about the size of my ass.

I don't want to think that I've bought into some ridiculous ideal, but maybe I have. Maybe giving up real sour cream for 1% less body fat isn't worth it. Maybe trading lasagna for cottage cheese is too high a price to pay for being able to wear a bathing suit in public. I know for a fact that none of it makes me a better person.

But I still can't quite bring myself to eat that M&M.

WISHFUL THINKING

I discovered recently that my mother doesn't know that I'm gay.

Really, I think it might be more accurate to say that she seems to have *forgotten* that I'm gay. Because I don't see how she could possibly not know. But she's pretending to.

I found out about this when she called my sister, Karen, and, during the course of an otherwise standard conversation, suddenly asked if I was dating any nice girls. Karen, slightly confused, said that no, she didn't think I was dating any nice girls.

"That's strange," my mother said. "He used to have so many nice girlfriends."

This part is true. I did use to have nice girlfriends. I even, briefly, got myself engaged to one of them in a weird kind of way. But we spent more time shopping together than we did making out, and even when I had my tongue in her mouth and my hand up her shirt I was thinking about how much nicer it would be to be doing the same thing with my baseball-player roommate.

Anyway, that was a long time ago. I haven't pitched woo with a woman since college, and I'm sure my mother must have noticed at some point that I was passing into my third decade with no apparent wedding plans. And even if she didn't, I've written a number of gay-themed books, some of which she's seen. So this sudden cluelessness thing baffles me.

I think maybe it's because, until recently, I hadn't dated in a long time. And she doesn't know about my new boyfriend because she and I don't talk all that much. So perhaps she just thinks that because so much time went by without me seeing anyone that I forgot I was gay, and if no one brings it up, I'll start dating girls again. She did the same thing when I was a kid and periodically announced that I was going to be something outlandish when I grew up, like a rodeo clown or one of the Rockettes. She just smiled and nodded, then never said a word about it again. Eventually I would forget all about whatever it was I wanted so badly to be and move on to something else, something she hoped was more appropriate. I think she's hoping I've moved on yet again.

No one in my family ever talks about anything personal, so on the one hand it's really not shocking that this subject has never come up. But the thing is, I was sure that we had addressed it in our own special way. Besides the books I've written, there was a conversation we had about religion in which I am sure I outed myself to my mother. I've even written about it, for heaven's sake, so it must be true.

But not to hear her tell it. She still seems to be waiting for me to settle down with a nice woman. So now I'm in a quandary. Part of me is thrilled that I now have a chance to out myself to a major figure in my life. I've never really gotten to do that before, primarily because no one I know really gives a rat's ass about such things. My father certainly didn't. None of my friends did. I guess my girlfriend in college was a little upset when she found out, but only because, she said, she hated it when her mother was right about her boyfriends.

Now I finally have an opportunity to shock someone. I've dreamed about such a moment for years. But the thing is, now that it's here, I don't think I really care anymore. In fact, in a lot of ways I resent having to come out at all to anyone. Why is it any of their business what I am or what I do? Why do we as gay people get stuck with having to *explain* ourselves to the people in our lives? They don't have to justify to us why they love the people they love. Why should we?

So I think what I'm going to do is not say a word. Sure, it would be fun to call mom up and say, "Hey, I hear you were asking after my girlfriends. Well, guess what? I have a boyfriend now. How do you like them apples?"

But I know what she'd do. She'd pretend I didn't say it. That's our family's way. A friend of mine calls it Baptist Selective Memory. That's where you look straight at the obvious and insist it's something different. "It's too bad about Uncle Henry being such a raging alcoholic," you might say, and Mom will look at you, smile, and reply, "Oh, honey, he just acts that way because he was struck by lightning during that big storm in '65. You know that." "Too bad about the Porter girl getting knocked up and having to go away" is countered with "Isn't it wonderful that little Lou-Ann Porter can be an exchange student to France this summer? I asked her to bring me back a beret."

You can't fight this kind of mental illness, so you might as well join it. I used to think that when I settled down with the man I loved I would want to take him home just to show the family that I could do it, that gay men, period, could do it. But now that I'm with a guy who seems a more-than-likely candidate for happily ever after, I see no reason to subject him to being called "Mike's special friend" and being asked if *he* is seeing any nice girls. Instead of trying to explain to my mother or to anyone else in my family that I happen to be a man who loves men, I think I'm just going to let those who don't want to acknowledge it keep wondering. Or, even better, they can make up their own reasons for what they see as my ongoing bachelorhood. "Is Mike gay?" someone will ask my mother eventually. "Oh, no," she'll say. "Don't you remember that big storm in '82?"

No Apologies

On March 12, 2000, Pope John Paul II led what he called "The Day of Pardon Mass" in St. Peter's Basilica. During the service, five Vatican cardinals and two bishops made confessions of sins that the Roman Catholic Church as an entity has committed over the years, with the pope then asking forgiveness from God for these accumulated actions.

Among the groups the church leaders admitted to wronging were Jews, gypsies, and other ethnic groups, as well as women and children. The pope, in a statement about the apologies, said he hoped that by publicly confessing before God, the Catholic Church can begin to heal the wounds it has caused and learn to love and respect people of all beliefs.

Apologizing has become very popular. Bill Clinton apologized to the American public for letting Monica Lewinsky blow him and then lying about it. The United States government has apologized to African-Americans for the infamous Tuskegee experiments, in which almost 400 black men with syphilis went untreated, and to Native Americans for stealing their land and trying to kill them off. The Swiss banking establishment apologized to victims of the Holocaust for helping the Nazis launder more than $94 million taken from Jewish families. It seems every time you turn around someone is apologizing for something.

I'm tired of people apologizing. Apologies don't cost anything. All they do is make the person doing the apologizing feel as if everything is even, while the person or people who have been wronged are still pretty much screwed.

Take the Native Americans. It's all well and good to say you're sorry about those smallpox-infested blankets, but that doesn't do anything to repair the damage done by the mistreatment of native cultures. I'd be more impressed if the government announced that as of the following morning, the only people allowed to live in North Dakota, Wyoming, and Oklahoma were the descendants of the people who lived there in the first place, or at least that Minnesota's Mall of America would be demolished so that the sacred land on which it sits won't have to suffer the further indignation of being invaded every minute of every day by idiots looking for another pair of shorts at the Gap.

The Swiss banks are no better. They wouldn't have apologized at all if they hadn't been forced to by the courts. And even if they agreed to return every single penny from every single account to its rightful owners, no amount of money can bring back entire families. After keeping that money for 50 years and then trying to cover up their involvement in the atrocities of the Holocaust, I think the truly just thing would be for every bank that accepted what they knew to be stolen funds to turn over their entire profits since World War II to some kind of fund set up to aid victims of genocides still occurring.

As for the Catholic Church, there's a lot more they could do to make it up to everyone they've stepped on if they really wanted to. We're talking about the wealthiest institution in the world. Forget the pope's apologies. I think it's time the Vatican became a homeless shelter. And then it's time to start writing some checks. They can start by sending a big one to every kid who was ever mistreated by a priest or a nun and made to feel like crap, or who was molested and told that telling about it was a sin. Then the church can move on to those who were told they weren't welcome because they were different or who died alone and ashamed because the church turned its back on them.

There are approximately 1.3 billion Catholics in the world. Even if the church paid each and every one of them a couple hundred bucks, they'd still have enough left over to put the pope into a retirement home. And maybe that's how it should be. Maybe starting over should mean going back to the very beginning. Maybe the Catholic Church needs to go back to what it was when it was founded, a group of poor people helping other poor people. Not a group of privileged old men who live in splendor and think they can atone for the damage their church has done for centuries by uttering a few apologies.

When I was a kid, my grandmother lived in a house next to ours. On nights when there was something on television that I wanted to watch and my parents wanted to watch something else, I would go over to my grandmother's and watch it there. One night I wanted to watch the movie *Jaws.* But my grandmother and I had had some kind of an argument that day, and she was angry with me. I knew I had to apologize if I wanted to see the movie. But I really didn't want to do it, probably because I knew that I was in the wrong.

I waited until the absolute last minute. Then I went

over, knocked on her door, and said I was sorry in the sweetest voice I could muster. My grandmother looked at me for a minute and then said, "That's not good enough. Come back when you've mowed the lawn." Then she shut the door.

Someday someone is going to apologize to the gay community for the way we've been treated over the years. Someday some government official or church figure is going to admit publicly that they were wrong, and they're going to ask us to forgive them. When they do, I hope we're able to look them in the eye and tell them to get back to us with a better offer.

So You Want to Be a Leatherman

There's something about leather. Maybe it's the smell. Or the look. Or the way it feels when your face is rubbing against someone's boot while he...oh, you know what I mean. Leather is just cool.

But not everyone can pull it off. Leather chaps on one guy look hot, while on another they look like some sort of cowboy outfit gone terribly wrong. A man who knows how to wear leather commands respect and inspires lust, while a man who doesn't just makes you start humming "Y.M.C.A."

What's the difference? Attitude. To be a successful leatherman, you have to *believe* that you can pull it off. So before you go pulling on those boots and strapping yourself into that harness, run through the following questions and find out if leather is right for you.

1. To you, "Gates of Hell" means:
   (a) A Dario Argento film
   (b) The latest hit video game
   (c) A cunning device that looks best on very large penises

2. The best thing for polishing leather is:
   (a) A damp rag
   (b) A damp tongue
   (c) A damp sheepskin

3. "Daddy knows best" is:
   (a) Your motto
   (b) A delightful 1950s television program
   (c) A damn lie

4. The best way to treat someone who's crying out in pain is to:
   (a) Speak in a reassuring tone to calm him down
   (b) Stuff a jock in his mouth to keep him quiet
   (c) Call a doctor

5. To you the abbreviations TT, FF, and WS are:
   (a) Meaningless
   (b) Warning signs
   (c) Turn-ons

6. Spitting is:
   (a) Foreplay
   (b) Rude
   (c) Unsanitary

7. Complete the line "These boots are made for _____"
   (a) Walking
   (b) Licking
   (c) Dancing

8. Your favorite kind of collar is:
   (a) Button-down
   (b) Peter Pan
   (c) Spiked

9. Which of the following is a term of endearment:
   (a) Sweetie
   (b) Honey
   (c) Hole

10. Your idea of the perfect boyfriend is:
    (a) Mr. Benson
    (b) Mr. Clean
    (c) Mr. Ed

ANSWERS:

1. (c)
2. (b)
3. (a)
4. (b)
5. (c)
6. (a)
7. (b)
8. (c)
9. (c)
10. (a)

SCORING:

Give yourself five points for each correct answer.

01–10: Forget leather; you can't even handle Saran Wrap. Stick with your chinos and sweaters, because touching leather would probably make you break out in hives. I bet you don't eat meat either.

15–20: OK, so you have a leather wallet. This does not a leather daddy make. If you want to butch it up a little, you might try buying a pair of motorcycle boots. But don't expect anyone to be licking them until you learn a few things about taking charge.

25–30: All right, *your* wallet is at least on a chain. I bet your nipple rings are too. You've seen at least one end of a sling in your lifetime, but you probably aren't ready to commit to this leather thing full time. That's OK. You look good in that harness, and that's what counts.

35–40: You likely have already made plans to attend the Folsom Street Fair. Your leather gear is handmade, not bought off the rack, and you know you look good in it. A few more turns around the block and you'll be looking to take your first IML title.

45–50: Yes, sir! Are your boots clean enough, sir?

Invisible Ink

I'm having my tattoos removed.

I have quite a few tattoos. People seldom believe this, because mostly they're covered up by clothes, but I do. I had the first one done over a decade ago, but I remember it like it was yesterday. Getting a tattoo in New York was still technically illegal at that time, a holdover from some public health scare during which the city banned tattooing to prevent the spread of hepatitis. Tattoo artists weren't allowed to hang out shingles, although they could advertise in the city's numerous alternative papers. I found mine in *The Village Voice*. I think I called her and hung up half a dozen times before I finally made my appointment.

When I was growing up tattoos were only for bikers and sailors. I remember seeing some of the older men in town with fuzzy greenish images on their forearms, the original designs of anchors and eagles now smeared into almost unrecognizable blurs. Even faded, there was something mysterious about them, something that spoke to me of adventure and mystery. Then there were the ones sported by younger men—men who drove motorcycles and generally behaved badly. Their tattoos were fresh and new, vibrant images painted on their bodies like warning signs.

I don't remember what exactly moved me to get my first tattoo. But I remember getting it. I can recall exactly how it felt sitting in the chair while a needle etched a picture into my body. It was, in many ways, a spiritual experience. The image reflected how I was feeling at the time, and it was a visible marker of my growth. I also thought it was cool.

Since then I've had four more tattoos, each one marking a particular moment in my life. I've enjoyed getting each one, and each one means something to me. But I don't need them any more. I don't know why, really, except that one day I was looking at them in the mirror and I realized it was time for them to go.

So now, once a month, I go to the dermatologist and lie on a table while he takes the tattoos off with a laser. Because we're doing all of my tattoos at once, this takes a while. I have a lot of time, as he moves the laser over my skin, to think about it what it all means.

My first tattoo was of the White Rabbit from *Alice in Wonderland*. I've always been a lot like the White Rabbit, and I thought he would make a good talisman. The woman who inked him onto my shoulder was used to doing things like burning skulls and naked women, and she thought my rabbit was great. She even had me model him in a tattoo show when it was all over. A year later, when I told her I wanted another tat, she suggested doing the same rabbit, only in a very butch motorcycle jacket and boots. She thought it symbolized the two sides of my personality, kind of a gay-boy yin/yang thing. I agreed, and on went the rebel rabbit, back to back with his more refined waistcoat-wearing, umbrella-toting twin.

Now the White Rabbit and his brother are being burned off my shoulder. One laser burst at a time, their lines of ink are being broken into small bits that my lymph system gobbles up and swallows. Tattoo removal is a long, painful process. The laser only takes away so much ink each time, and you need to wait a while between treatments. It will take me about six months to be wiped clean, like a blackboard removed of chalk.

Right now my rabbits are about half gone, ghostly reflections of their former selves. When I look at them in the mirror, I see them just below the surface, as if they're staring up at me from under water. While from a monetary and pain management standpoint I would prefer it if one treatment wiped away all signs of the tattoos, I kind of like this gradual goodbye. I've lived with these pictures for so long that I don't remember what I look like without them. This way, I have time to get used to the idea.

When someone asks me to describe what getting a tattoo is like, I can't really do it. I can tell them that it sort of feels like having a pin dragged along your skin repeatedly. But that's inadequate. I can't explain that the rest of it, the wonderful part, is feeling something being written on your body, a visual record of who you are at that particular moment in your life. I can't really explain how having to trust someone to paint your skin with a steel needle and colored inks is one of the most intimate moments you can experience. All I can tell them is that it kind of hurts, but in a magical way.

Similarly, I can't really explain how having my tattoos removed feels. I can tell you that the physical pain of being burned with a laser is like being snapped with a rubber band repeatedly. In doing research on tattoo removal, I found one source that described the pain as being splattered with bacon grease. While hardly encouraging, this is a fitting description, but mainly because the smell really does remind me of bacon cooking. The other day, while undergoing another treatment, I sniffed the air and had the sudden, horrible, realization that the only thing that really keeps humans from becoming someone's breakfast is the fact that pigs can't manipulate machinery.

But the physical pain is only part of the process. The real work is in saying goodbye to the person you used to be. When I called to make my first appointment for laser surgery, the nurse said, "So it's time to grow up, is it?" I knew what she meant, but she's got it all wrong. This isn't about growing up. It's about continuing the journey. I'm not having my tattoos removed because I don't like them or because they stand in the way of my getting a job. I'm having them removed because just as it was important for me to get them in the first place, it's now important for me to reclaim the space they occupy. I want my skin back. It's part of an overall process of reclaiming my body, which is important to me right now.

But even when they're gone, the ink turned into invisible particles eaten by my system, my tattoos will still be there. I will remember how it felt to get them, how it felt when someone rubbed his hands over them admiring them, and how it felt having them removed. Each of these memories is meaningful to me, and I don't want to forget them. There is pain in memory, but there is also joy. So as the laser zaps my skin and the White Rabbit and the other tattoos grow fainter and fainter, it's with a mixture of sadness and relief that I let them go.

I just wish I smelled less like bacon frying and more like a Pop-Tart toasting.

DRESS REHEARSAL

This morning I spent a good hour or so crying over the death of my dog, Roger. I recalled how hard it had been to make the decision, how difficult to put him in the car one last time, helping him in because his legs weren't working right anymore. I saw his face, gray with age, as he sniffed at the open window, taking in the smell of the ocean as we drove to the vet. And then, worst of all, I remembered holding him as the vet asked, "Are you sure?" and I looked into Roger's big, trusting brown eyes and nodded, playing God. Moments later it was over, and I cradled his great lifeless body in my arms and wept.

It felt good to cry, to let out all of the unhappiness and guilt and rage. When it was over, I felt cleansed, as if I'd just taken a shower or had my teeth cleaned. The only problem was, Roger wasn't dead. He was sitting on the floor beside my desk, very much alive, looking at me with a puzzled expression that clearly indicated that he was wondering if this time I'd finally lost it for good and he'd have to find someone else to take him for his afternoon walk.

It will probably be a number of years before Roger really does kick off. He's only 8, and apart from a gimpy leg he's in good health. But sometimes I look at him and imagine the worst. Many of his dog friends have died this year, mostly from cancers of one kind or another, and part of me is firmly convinced that he's next on the list. I check him frequently for lumps and worry when he stumbles while walking or doesn't seem to get up as quickly as he used to.

That's when the dress rehearsal begins. I start to imagine the inevitable, not just as a passing thought, but in full glorious detail. I revel in describing to myself the way things look and feel and smell, the way I will react to them and the way I will be affected by them. I savor each moment, letting it melt over my mind like chocolate sauce over ice cream, soaking me in its peculiar pleasure, making me high with its sweetness. By the time I'm finished, I'm frequently convinced that whatever it is I've been imagining has really happened.

Recently I found myself in a time of exceptionally high stress involving work. I had two enormous concurrent deadlines, and neither was being met with anything even remotely resembling professionalism or timeliness. The editors involved were becoming testy, and I was becoming more and more unable to write a word without feeling sick.

Finally, and without warning, my body went on strike. One afternoon, as I was frantically attempting to write two books at once, I found that I couldn't speak. Not a word. I could get a few sounds out if I really pushed, but mostly they were just sad little raspy noises, like a death rattle. I sounded like Old Yeller in his last hours.

Shortly thereafter I began to have trouble breathing. My chest had tightened up, and I felt as if I'd swallowed enormous quantities of water. It wasn't painful, exactly, but I had the distinct impression that I was drowning.

Now, a normal person (i.e., someone who is not a writer) would have done something sensible at this point, like go immediately to a doctor or emergency room. Did I do this? Of course not. I stretched out on the bed and *imagined* going to the doctor. I imagined him looking down my throat with great interest, then gazing at me sadly and saying, "I hate to tell you this, but you're probably going to die very soon. And badly. It won't be pretty. Would you like me to load you up with morphine now, or would you like to wait until the pain really kicks in?"

I replayed this scenario with several different endings. In some I was diagnosed with cancer, resulting in months of treatment and a final, pale death while my boyfriend held my hand and my loved ones cried uncontrollably. In others I ended up with black lung or malaria or typhoid—something vaguely exotic that I would be able to describe vividly to all of my friends. ("The pain is like breathing in *fire.*") And sometimes I just saw myself dropping dead right on the spot, crumpled on the floor for someone to discover after trying to reach me on the phone for two days.

Now, I have had friends and loved ones who really have died in these various ways (well, perhaps not exactly from malaria or typhoid, but you get the idea), and I know they are not pleasant ways to go, not even remotely. But when I'm engaged in Let's Pretend, they all seem wildly glamorous, rife with possibilities for drama and pathos, not to mention opportunities to make everyone around me feel sorry for me.

Finally I *did* discover the source of my sudden muteness and my breathing difficulties. It was, the doctor informed me, a combination of stress and the return of a chest infection I'd picked up a number of years ago while on my first book tour. This was far less exciting than the other possibilities I'd considered, but was not without potential. The chest thing, for example, was pleurisy. By itself pleurisy is not all that fascinating; it's simply the inflammation of the lining of the chest cavity. However, it's rarely seen in people under the age of, oh, 70 or 80. When it was first diagnosed, my doctor had looked at me skeptically and said, "How old did you say you are?"

Having pleurisy was a bonus because it let me think that maybe, just maybe, there was something wrong with my insides. Somehow my 30-something body had a 70-something disease. This was cause for celebration. After all, if pleurisy had me in its grip, surely rheumatism and Alzheimer's couldn't be far behind.

Even more thrilling was the idea that I had gone mute from *stress*. Who would ever think such a wonderful thing could happen? Why, I felt just like Janet Jackson, who I'd recently read had been hospitalized for fatigue and nervousness. How glorious to be so busy, so overworked, so *frantic* that my body had to revolt and refuse to work. It was, I thought, quite an achievement.

The doctor assured me that my voice would come back when it was ready, probably in a few days. I nodded happily, not listening to a word. I was too busy wondering how long it would take me to master sign language, and thinking about how all of my faraway friends would now only be able to contact me by mail. True, it was a little sad to think of never singing or talking again, but it seemed a small price to pay for the privilege of being the guy who went mute from stress.

Of course my voice did come back, slowly and froggily, so that at first I sounded like Mercedes McCambridge, then Hermione Gingold, and finally Brenda Vaccaro before returning to my old self. But by that time I'd moved on to something else anyway, and it was a relief to be able to answer the phone and not sound like that guy who terrorizes the baby-sitter in *Are You in the House Alone?*

I have a surprising number of friends who have planned their own funerals, and in astonishing detail. Two of them meet regularly to discuss what they've come up with, making elaborate notes on everything from the month during which they hope to pass on (February is a strong favorite) to the music they want played (no Celine Dion seems to be a point of agreement among all involved). They've come up with menus for the party afterward as well as written statements they wish to be read to the assembled guests. They keep all these things in notebooks, along with instructions for what they want inscribed on their tombstones and how to divvy up their collections of Fiesta ware and Dusty Springfield CDs.

You might think this sort of thing would be right up my alley, but it isn't. Despite the fact that in high school, when we were creating a mock community and appointing people to various positions of power, I was unanimously chosen the village undertaker, I am not all that enamored of death. I mean, thinking about my own has its moments, but it's more *how* one dies that sends a shiver of excitement down my spine than the whole funeral thing.

I'm much happier when imaging things that will have repercussions in the present. For instance, I am quite fond of thinking about what could happen if I were to run into one of my boyfriend's exes. It will probably not come as a great shock to many to learn that I am capable of harboring unreasonable and occasionally perhaps just the tiniest bit psychotic resentment of men my partner has been with before me. This is, perhaps, why he allows me to believe that he met me mere seconds after exiting the doors of a monastery in which he had been cloistered since birth.

Despite his best efforts, however, there are moments when I am made aware that this is not the case. For example, several weeks ago, while walking home from a perfectly enjoyable dinner, my boyfriend and I ran into a man who engaged us in conversation. To be more precise, he engaged my boyfriend in conversation while I stood by and watched. It became clear to me that this man and my boyfriend had at some point had a history, a deduction made possible primarily by the fact that I was not introduced and that upon the resumption of our walk home, the subject of the man's identity was mysteriously avoided in favor of a discussion about the beauty of the moon (which was behind the clouds) and the loveliness of the evening (which was unseasonably chilly).

This was all I needed. For the next week I entertained thoughts of murder. As it turned out, the man we'd run into lived only a block away. I saw him frequently. And each time I did I imagined newer and bloodier ways of bringing about, if not his death, at least his total and very public humiliation. My favorite scenario (and there were many) involved running into him at a bar, where he would say something that justified my smacking him across the nose with a beer bottle before beating him into a screaming stain. Being taken away by police for my behavior was a happy, if not entirely necessary, addendum to the fantasy.

This man, of course, had no idea that I hated him.

Whenever he saw me he smiled pleasantly, going about his business as if he wasn't at the very top of my personal 10 Most Wanted list. And if I ever *had* run into him in a bar, I'm sure that I wouldn't have done anything even remotely like try to kill him. Probably. Almost certainly.

But it was fun to think about. And that, after all, is the whole point of the dress rehearsal. It allows you to get out all of those feelings that you really probably shouldn't allow to have free rein in reality. It's all well and good to imagine yourself receiving the news that you have only two days to live. It's even OK to enjoy the dark little happiness it brings you. But probably if this were to really happen to you, things wouldn't be quite so nice. Similarly, it can be great fun to think about slipping just the merest pinch of, say, arsenic into the chicken Caesar salad of the reviewer who trashed your last book. But most of us are not really going to do these things. *Most* of us. On *good* days.

Sometimes I worry that all of this weirdness, this twisted little inner life of mine, will seep out into the real world and everyone will see me for who I am—Wednesday Addams with a dick. Probably it's too late for that anyway. I know that there are definitely times when, interrupted during one of my dress rehearsals, I'm pulled back into the real world still holding onto a scrap of whatever bizarre scene I was acting out. I've held Roger and told him what a good, good boy he is after moments before feeling deeply his last moments on earth. I've picked up the jangling telephone only to find myself talking to the very editor who, minutes earlier, I was shoving from the top of a very high building. At times like these, things can get a little dicey.

But mostly I'm OK. I've yet to actually poison anyone's salad or stab somebody's hand with a dinner fork.
But you never know. At least, should I ever really get that
bad news from my doctor or find myself facing the electric
chair, I'll know my lines.

Against All Odds

I've been thinking a lot about relationships lately. My boyfriend and I are coming up on an anniversary, and it amazes me that I'm able to say that. Actually, what amazes me is that relationships happen at all. I mean, think about it. There are so many things that need to fall into place for two people to get together. Especially two gay people. We aren't like heterosexuals—who can just assume that anyone of the opposite sex might be a potential partner. Just because we see a guy or a girl we like, it doesn't mean we have a chance. Assuming said person is single, we have to then hope that he or she is gay—which isn't the case nearly as often as most of us would like.

And once that gigantic hurdle is cleared, we still have all the other potential relationship-killers to face. Not only do we have to be attracted to another person, but the other person has to be attracted back. That's no small feat. There are a million things that could go wrong. Maybe he won't like your receding hairline. Maybe you won't like his teeth. We all have those weird little things we like and don't like. A negative response to any one of them could signal an immediate end to the whole thing.

Assuming each of you finds the other attractive, you then have to move on to the personality issue. What if that guy you spot is single and gay, happens to be your type and likes the type you are, but he's the most boring conversationalist you've ever had to endure? Or suppose you like to stay in on the weekends while he wants to go out partying? Honestly, the odds of any two people matching up all the way to this point are so small as to be staggering. Yet we manage it. Sometimes.

And none of this even begins to touch on all the other things that need to be worked out in a relationship, like career compatibility, sexual needs, pet preferences, television remote control issues, and whether to hang the toilet paper so that it comes over or under. Once you factor in all these things, you might as well give up and start thinking nice thoughts about single life.

But we don't. We insist on trying. Like those sad little salmon valiantly flinging themselves upstream to spawn, we throw ourselves into the relationship fray over and over and over, hoping to land our perfect match. We refuse to face the mathematical evidence proving that finding a compatible partner is less likely than being killed by flying sideshow freaks during a tornado that sweeps through a traveling carnival and carries them halfway across the country before dropping them on our heads with a sad little thump.

When I think about everything that had to line up for my boyfriend and me to meet, it makes my stomach tight because I realize that at every step of the way one tiny misalignment could have blown the whole deal. Along with the usual requirements, the two of us also needed the help of a well-timed cross-country move, simultaneous recoveries from the end of previous relationships, and the brilliance of a mutual friend. The chances of these things all occurring in the required order, at the right time, with the necessary results, are far too remote to even consider.

When I think that just one thing not going right could have resulted in one or both of us dating someone else, I get nauseous.

Then again, I suppose one little change could have resulted in one or both of us dating Bruce Willis. But that's not the point. The point is that this is all really weird. I feel like anyone who does manage to get into a relationship that works and makes them happy should feel as if they've cheated the fates. There are a lot of forces working against us when it comes to finding love, and it's not as if we're getting a lot of help out there. We have to do the best we can with what we've got, and when it works, I think we deserve to celebrate a little.

But do we? Do we celebrate one another's relationships? Not really. In fact, I think a lot of us look at long-term gay relationships with suspicion. "Why have those two been together so long?" we wonder. "I bet he's only with him for his money." Or for the sex or because he's scared of being alone or because of any other excuse we can think of, except, of course, that maybe, just maybe, they're together because they've made it work.

We don't have relationship models as gay people. No one tells us how it can work. All we have to go on is what the heterosexuals we grow up around have, and quite frankly, most of them have made a mess of things. So we know we don't want to be like them, but we don't know what the other options are. And it's not like we get a chance to practice. We don't generally get to date as teenagers like heteros do, and when you think about it, teenage dating is nothing more than training for adult relationships. It's relationship boot camp, where you get to make mistakes and try different tactical maneuvers to see what works and what doesn't. Then, when you grow up and start playing for keeps, you have at least a basic idea of how it works.

Gay people don't have that. We don't get any training. We pretty much sit around confused and frustrated until we're old enough to go out on our own and start dating. Then we're supposed to know what to do, and most of us don't. We're 21 or 25 or 30 and we feel like we're 13 as far as relating to other people sexually and emotionally.

No wonder so many of our relationships fail. I know, we aren't supposed to talk about that because it's what the right-wingers accuse us of so often. But it's true a lot of the time. We really don't know what we're doing. I didn't when I started dating. I was so happy to finally be touching other men that I thought it would all sort itself out and come naturally, like when baby penguins are pushed into the water and know exactly how to swim.

But it didn't work that way. It was hard. Really hard. I floundered. And after a decade of practice, it's still hard, even though I've learned enough to keep my head above water most of the time. I still don't have a rule book, and my boyfriend and I are pretty much making it up as we go along. We know we don't want what our parents had or what most of our friends have, so we're trying to come up with something different. That's why, as our anniversary approaches and I think about what it took to get us this far, I keep looking up in the sky, wondering just when those sideshow freaks are going to drop on me.

Happily Ever After

I never thought I'd be saying this, but I watched a movie last night starring Meg Ryan and Tom Hanks — and I liked it. It was late, I was flipping through the channels aimlessly, and there it was: *You've Got Mail,* a film I was sure would make me retch. But it was that or reruns of *The Brady Bunch* on Nick at Nite. You can only watch Marcia's nose get broken by that football so many times, so I decided to take a chance on Meg and Tom.

Much to my surprise, it was charming. Of course, it had the advantage of being based on the wonderful 1940 Jimmy Stewart film *The Shop Around the Corner,* which was made at a time when people still knew how to make charming films. Still, even in its updated version it managed to retain something that very few films these days have: It made me believe in romance.

I know, I always complain that romance is dead. Well, it is, especially in the movies that pass for romantic comedies these days. Gone are films like *It Happened One Night* and *The Philadelphia Story,* movies that had you really hoping the main characters would get together by the end of the picture. Now we just have anxiety-ridden star vehicles where we're forced to watch the characters undergo 90 minutes of therapy while they try to figure out why they can't commit to one another and decide they're better off single. Let's face it, the last movie that really gave us a good romantic ending featured Julia Roberts as a hooker doing

Richard Gere a favor. Hardly the stuff of fairy tales.

Perhaps I was particularly susceptible to *You've Got Mail* because I'd just come from a screening at my local queer film festival of a movie that was anything but romantic. I won't embarrass the creator by naming the film. I will just say that it was a painful, not very original look at the demise of a dysfunctional gay relationship. It was one of those movies where you hate all the characters, don't want any of them to end up happy, and feel the need to shower immediately upon returning home because everyone in the film smoked too much.

As I watched Tom and Meg doing their courtship dance, I found myself wondering why all of the queer films I've ever seen about relationships are so depressing. I couldn't think of one of the many I've watched over the years where I felt a sense of hope at the end, a feeling of happiness because the characters really seemed to enjoy being in love and losing themselves in the joy of being together. Instead, they all seem to be about how dismal it is trying to find someone to love.

This surprises me. As a rule, gay audiences go wild for those old romantic comedies. At least most of the guys I know do. We love to see other people's lives turn out well. But not, apparently, our own lives. The films we make about gay romance tend to be bleak, filled with one-night stands who never call back, boyfriends who cheat, and lots and lots of drinking.

I think *Jeffrey* was supposed to be a romantic comedy, but it came off more as a farce than anything heartwarming. And *Love! Valour! Compassion!* was sweet in its way, although it didn't exactly leave me with a warm fuzzy feeling. The closest gay cinema has come to creating anything truly like an old-fashioned romantic comedy is 1999's *Trick*. But it was hard to become caught up in the trials and tribulations of two guys searching for a place to get off. Although the film tries to redeem itself with a sweet, nonsexual ending, it was too little, too late. After all, a stripper nicknamed "Beer Can" is no match for Cary Grant.

My friend Jeff says there will never be a true queer romantic comedy because only straight people still fall for the notion of happily ever after. He thinks gay filmmakers opt for bitterness over sentimentality because it's more realistic. "Watching two guys looking for a place to have sex is a lot more believable than watching them do a courtship dance," says Jeff. "It's probably because we know that even if they do fall in love, one of them will leave the other for a guy he meets at the gym six months later."

That does indeed seem to be the basic message of most gay films about relationships. But is it because we really aren't good at romance, or is it because it's easier to jump straight to the bitterness and save ourselves the risk of getting hurt by trying something else? Maybe it's time we gave romance another try. After all, if Tom and Meg can do it, so can we.

On My Own

A couple of months ago, while talking to my friend Scott, I mentioned that I had gone to a movie the night before.

"Who'd you go with?" he asked.

"No one," I said. "I went by myself."

There was a long pause. "On a Friday night?" Scott said.

"Yes," I answered. "On a Friday night. Why?"

"That's date night," Scott said. "I would never go to a movie alone, but especially not on date night."

This had never occurred to me. "Why not?" I asked.

Scott sighed. "Do you want everyone to think you're a loser?" he said, as if explaining to a child that you don't stick knives into electrical outlets.

"Look," I said. "None of my friends wanted to see this, and I needed to get out of the house. Why wouldn't I go?"

"It's your life," said Scott, clearly horrified to know me.

After this exchange, I started asking my other friends if they ever went to movies alone. I couldn't believe I was the only one who didn't think it was strange to see a film solo.

"Absolutely not," my friend Anna said when I asked if she would ever go by herself. "Have you ever seen the people who go to movies alone? They're creepy. Whenever I see someone sitting alone at a theater I assume he's either jacking off or crazy—or both."

My other friends were even less help. "I'll go if I absolutely can't get anyone else to come," said Lily. "But I make sure I go to a matinee because there are fewer people there and there's less chance of running into someone who recognizes me. And I take a notebook and pretend to write in it so people will think I'm reviewing the film or something."

"I've done it a few times," Jim said when I asked him if he would go. "But I always buy two tickets so everyone will think I'm waiting for a date."

Out of all my friends, only one admits to regularly going to movies alone, and she only does it because she can't stand to have anyone talk to her while she's watching the film. The rest find the idea absolutely horrifying. For whatever reason, they see going to a movie by themselves as a desperate act. They're convinced that everyone will think they have no friends. Never mind that they'd be in a dark place with dozens of other people who wouldn't even see their faces. They can't bear the idea of even walking in and out of a theater unaccompanied.

I've never understood this fear of being alone. I spend most of my life trying to avoid other people, so the idea of actually being by myself from time to time is heavenly. But I have many friends who can't stand the idea. They always have significant others in their lives, even if they don't really like them, because being single makes them tense and nervous. The idea of going to a movie or to dinner or, worst of all, traveling alone is enough to send them into a meltdown.

Gay men are particularly paranoid about doing anything by themselves. It's like we're all descended from hye-

nas or something and need to live in packs or face extinc-
tion. We go out in groups. We travel in groups. We work
out in groups. We even—at least some of us—have sex in
groups. A gay man out and about alone is about as rare as
a glimpse of Halley's comet.

Where did this idea come from that being single—or
being perceived as being single—is shameful? Why would
we rather not do something enjoyable than do it alone?
When I told my friends that I was dating someone, they
breathed a collective sign of relief. "Finally, you'll have
someone to do stuff with," they said. "Now we don't have
to worry about you."

Apparently all this time that I've been enjoying life by
myself I was in desperate need of a chaperone. I guess I
should consider myself lucky that I didn't do serious
injury to myself while I was carelessly sitting in theaters
alone and recklessly consuming lunches and dinners with
no one there to look out for my safety. And heaven knows
how all of those airplanes managed to stay in the sky while
I was sitting on them without anyone beside me. Surely it's
a miracle I'm still alive.

I hope my boyfriend realizes what an awesome task
he's undertaken. Rescuing me from the shame of buying a
single movie ticket is not a responsibility that should be
taken lightly. And I've definitely learned my lesson. Never
again will I venture into a restaurant by myself and tell the
waiter to have the chef make whatever he thinks would be
fun for me to try, lest everyone there assume that I have no
one in my life. No more will I purchase a single ticket to a
concert, even if it means giving up that choice seat in the
front row left available because everyone else bought

pairs. And gone are the days of taking last-minute trips to interesting places, because it's so much more fun to have to schedule everything months ahead of time and argue about the destination because that makes you feel like a couple.

Yes, I feel much, much better now that my days of being alone are over. But if one of these nights you happen to go to a movie and see someone sitting all by himself in the back row, please don't tell any of my friends. I told them I was too busy to go out with them.

FOR BETTER OR FOR WORSE

I did something recently that I rarely do—I changed my mind.

To be specific, I changed my mind about this whole gay marriage thing. I used to not be a fan of the idea. My feeling was that trying to be more like heterosexuals was really just driving us farther away from our queer identities. I thought that trying to legitimize our relationships by using their methods was admitting that they were right.

I still feel that way about marriage in general. I think turning what should be an emotional and spiritual commitment into a legal transaction is horrible, and the fact that we're essentially now engaged in a debate that centers around what kind of genitals two people forming a union have is pure stupidity.

But I've changed my mind anyway. What finally made me do it was the passage of California's infamous Proposition 22, which effectively bans the recognition of gay marriages—even if they occur elsewhere—in California. I wasn't surprised that the proposition passed, but I *was* surprised that so many queers voted in favor of it. A friend of mine who lives in California, talking about the vote, said, "I'm so glad it passed. Now those hets will realize that we don't want what they have."

In many ways, I respect that sentiment. But there's a

fatal flaw in the logic: You can't reject something you didn't have in the first place.

It's easy to say that you don't want to be like heterosexuals and to decry the institution of marriage. But when becoming a part of that institution is not even an option, rejecting it is an empty gesture. It's like telling a group of bigger, meaner kids who won't let you play ball with them that you didn't want to play anyway and you're going home. It may make *you* feel better about being excluded, but while you're sitting up in your room being self-righteously satisfied, they're having a great time playing ball and thinking they're better than you.

The fact is, you can't quit a club you didn't belong to in the first place. Because marriage as a legally-recognized institution has never been available to us as gay people, saying that we don't want it doesn't mean anything at all. And trying to look at the passage of Proposition 22 as some kind of victory for queer resistance is complete nonsense. All of those gay people who voted for it may think they were striking some kind of blow for radicalism, but millions of nongay people see the success of the anti–gay-marriage campaign as concrete proof that the majority of America doesn't want to see queers have the same rights that straights enjoy.

Truthfully, I would like to see marriage as a legal institution destroyed. I don't understand why people who choose to sign what is essentially a contract regarding shared property should receive any benefits. But they do, and that's not going to change. That means that the most powerful option available to us as gay people is to make sure we at least have the same legal opportunities that

straight couples do. Then, if we still want to make a statement by rejecting marriage, it will mean something. We
will actually be giving something up in exchange for keeping our principles.

It's very difficult for me to accept that becoming a little more like the mainstream I so much despise is really
taking a step forward. But it is. I think the reluctance I felt
for so long about accepting the validity of legally sanc-
tioned gay marriage was a response to years of being told
that I, as a gay man, wasn't welcome in a largely straight
world. Rather than try to change the way things are to
accommodate me, it was easier to say I didn't want them to
change anyway.

I think, though, that this is one of the most decep-
tive—and successful—tactics used by an oppressive
majority that wants to retain its position of power. By con-
tinuously pushing outsiders away, those in control convince the people they're trying to keep out of the inner circle that getting inside isn't a worthwhile goal anyway.
Eventually, what should be viewed as being wrongfully
excluded is turned around, and the oppressed group
begins to see itself as choosing to deliberately remain outside the majority. And once you accept that outsider status,
it becomes very easy to wear it as a badge of honor.

There's no honor in being excluded, though. There's
no pride in turning your back on equality just because
demanding it puts you on par with people or ideas you
don't respect. You need to have something in your posses-
sion before giving it away can free you from the responsibility of owning it.

Maybe I wouldn't marry the man I love if it were a

viable option. Maybe I would still reject marriage as an antiquated system of control. And maybe doing so would make me feel as if I'd made a stand against something. But until rejecting these things actually means turning my back on something I don't believe in, not marrying him is simply one more choice I don't have the right to make while other people do. And that pisses me off.

So You Want to Be a Drama Queen

In my opinion the phrase "drama queen" is used far too casually. Once reserved for truly special personages, it is now employed to describe anyone—gay or nongay—who exhibits the slightest sign of hysteria over any given situation. This is not acceptable. A real drama queen is far more than a nervous nelly. He (or she, depending on your choice of pronouns for your friends) manages to make *everything* about him (or her). This takes skill. The true drama queen does not simply demand attention, he (or she) *absorbs* it from every possible source. Only a genuine drama queen, for example, is able to convince all of his (or her) friends that the appearance of a former lover at a gay pride parade attended by 57,000 other people is a deliberately orchestrated slight or that the occurrence of a stain on a favorite shirt is most decidedly going to alter the course of life as we know it.

So before you go reaching for that Oscar after your latest melodramatic meltdown, take this handy quiz to determine whether you're truly a leading lady or simply a bit player.

1. Madonna is coming to town, but you are unable to obtain tickets to the show, even though you are the president of her local fan club, know every lyric by heart, and have already purchased the *exact same outfit* she wore in the "Ray of Light" video. You:

(a) Decide to sell everything you own in order to purchase tickets from a scalper

(b) Write her a scathing letter and send it accompanied by all of her CDs smashed into tiny pieces

(c) Enter a convent

2. It is the day of the annual White Party. Wanting to look your best, you go to the tanning salon. Unfortunately, you emerge slightly redder than you wanted to be. You:

(a) Call the friends you were supposed to go with, pretending to have come down with the flu, and tell them it is their duty to stay home with you and make you feel better

(b) Apply a great deal of bronzer to try to even out the color

(c) Reassure yourself that it will be very dark and that everyone will be too tweaked to notice anyway

3. While out with your friends on a Saturday night, you see a guy you slept with once six months ago who never called you again. But now you see him making out with another man. You:

(a) Ask your best-looking friend to make out with you in the other guy's line of vision

(b) Have another drink and forget about it

(c) Walk up to them, throw your drink in the one-time trick's face, and scream, "That's for giving me anal warts!"

4. You're shopping with a friend. While trying on some

cute black pants, you discover that you have to go from
a 30 waist to a 32. You:

(a) Demand to see a store manager and threaten to sue
the store for obviously mislabeling their merchan-
dise and causing you irreparable mental anguish

(b) Remind yourself that sizes do sometimes vary, and
that your other 30s still fit perfectly well

(c) Suck it in until you can button the pants and then
insist on buying them

5. You have a big birthday approaching—one that ends in
a 0. You react by:

(a) Not telling anyone

(b) Telling everyone so that they'll throw you a party

(c) Leaving a message on your best friend's answering
machine saying that you've just taken 150 sleeping
pills, then waiting for him to rush over so that you
can admit that it was just something you were con-
sidering doing and that he really didn't need to
trouble himself on your account

6. You've planned a brunch for 10 of your very best
friends. Just before they arrive you realize that you
don't have any Bloody Mary mix. You:

(a) Quickly call a friend and ask him to pick some up
on the way over

(b) Wait for the first guests to show up and open the
door while sobbing hysterically and wailing,
"Everything is ruined"

(c) Decide your friends drink too much and serve
them orange juice instead

7. It's your three-month anniversary with your current
   boyfriend. He makes no mention of it, even though
   you've dropped numerous hints. You:
   (a) Give him a card and a really nice present so that
       he'll feel guilty
   (b) Forget about it because he's a great guy
   (c) Go out and sleep with someone else, then call your
       boyfriend from the other guy's house and say, "If
       you really loved me, I wouldn't have to do things
       like this to get your attention."

8. You learn that your favorite brand of cologne is being
   discontinued. You:
   (a) Chain yourself to the fragrance counter at the
       department store and refuse to budge until you
       speak to Tommy himself
   (b) Buy up as many bottles as you can find, figuring it
       will last you at least a couple of years
   (c) Switch to a different kind because change is good

9. During a particularly enthusiastic sex session, your
   boyfriend gets oil-based lube on your very expensive
   sheets. You:
   (a) Don't mention it, because it's not every day that
       you get it so hard that you can't walk afterward
   (b) Call your friend who's into leather and ask him
       how he gets Crisco out of his sheets
   (c) Wrap the sheets around you like a shroud and
       keen for hours while your confused boyfriend
       repeatedly asks what's wrong

10. While preparing for your first date with a guy you've been dying to go out with for a long time, you just can't get your hair quite right. You:
   (a) Decide to wear a baseball cap and pretend you're going for the casual, sporty look
   (b) Decide that probably only you will know that not every single hair is in place and forget about it
   (c) Decide your life is over and cancel at the last minute, claiming a death in the family

ANSWERS:

1. (c)
2. (a)
3. (c)
4. (a)
5. (c)
6. (b)
7. (c)
8. (a)
9. (c)
10. (c)

SCORING:

Give yourself five points for each correct answer.

01–10: There's little or no drama in your life. We're not sure if this is a good thing or if it's sad.

15–20: Every so often you throw a royal temper tantrum,

but overall you're more of a lady-in-waiting than a drama queen.

25–30: You probably wanted to be Maria in your high school production of *West Side Story.* You didn't get the part, and now you're making up for it.

35–40: Your friends know you as Your Majesty, and normally they find your outbursts oddly charming. But don't start writing that Oscar acceptance speech quite yet. You need a few more star turns before you snatch that Best Actress trophy.

45–50: We'd present you with a scepter and crown—but you clearly already have them. All hail the queen!

THANK-YOU NOTE

This morning I had some tea. It was some kind of mixed berry tea, herbal because caffeine does weird things to me that makes me think I probably need to go to an emergency room. But the flavor is not important.

What is important is that I drank the tea out of a mug that was sent to me two years ago at Christmas by the literary agency that represents me. It's a plain white mug with a drawing of the building that houses the people who, like the Greek Fates, weave the thread of my career and, I am convinced, sit there with their golden shears ready to snip that thread at any moment. It probably cost them all of 85 cents per mug, and I recall vividly the thought that went through my head when I opened the little box and saw what was inside: *Well, this is clearly your last chance.*

I am convinced that the quality of the Christmas gift I receive from my agency is directly related to my worth to them. The first year I was with them, I received a lovely big box of apples and a cheery card welcoming me to the family. For weeks I chomped apples as I sat at my desk writing, sure that everything was going to be perfect now that I had someone who believed in me. The second year, when nothing I'd given my agent had sold, my Christmas gift was a strange little book that I suspect my agent plucked from a pile of review copies she had sitting around. There was a short, awkward, note in it that I took as a veiled threat to produce something or else.

When the mug came, I left it in its box and didn't look at it. It was too painful. It reminded me that I had yet to pay off for this big New York agency that had taken me on with such high expectations. Of course, this didn't stop me from putting the box on the kitchen counter, where I couldn't help but see it every time I had to open the cupboard or needed to clear space to chop something. Whenever I picked it up or moved it, I was reminded of my diminishing worth as a writer, of the painful fact that, as of that year, I was worth only an approximately 85-cent investment.

About two months ago, my roommate finally took the mug out of its box. He needed something to put paintbrushes in. He thought the mug would be perfect since, as he remarked casually, "You're not doing anything with it."

But I was doing something with it. I was letting it depress me. As a mug, it wasn't particularly pleasing to look at, but I got great satisfaction from knowing that it was there, like a sweet little cancer waiting to take over whatever space I allowed it to fill. Being forced to move it whenever I needed to tend to a basic physical need like eating allowed me the dark pleasure of handling a talisman of my failure, reminding me of everything that stood between me and receiving a really good Christmas gift, one of the gifts I imagined the agency's successful writers were all getting.

Now the mug was out of its box. There it sat, filled with murky water and an assortment of stained brushes. I passed it several times a day as I went in and out of the kitchen. Even though I tried not to, I glanced at it every time. And every time, that scab was ripped off again, and I would have the pleasure of thinking, for maybe half an hour, about how awful it was that I hated the things I was writing to make a living and how unfair it was that writing the things I loved wouldn't pay the rent. Once or twice, I considered knocking the mug onto the floor. But I knew I would have to pick up the broken pieces and mop the paint-muddied water off the linoleum. Part of me was attracted to this picture. Something else to be depressed about. Another indignity forced upon me by my lack of motivation. But then the mug would be gone. I left it where it was.

Along with my depression about the mug came another kind of depression, a darker and more oppressive one. At first I assumed it was just the general moodiness that I am subject to from time to time, a kind of overall grayness that sweeps in and clouds things for a couple of days. But when a week went by, and then another, and I was still depressed, I started to wonder.

True, I was under more stress than usual with work. True, I had been thinking lately that maybe I'd made a terrible mistake in choosing writing as a career. These were not new things, however. In fact, they're regular visitors, and over the years I've learned to recognize them, let them have their whiny, raucous stay, and then kick them out when even I can't stand the sound of their voices in my head anymore.

I knew I was really depressed because I'd stopped eating for the most part. I would pick at things here and there, but more and more I was going all day without putting anything in my mouth until, around 10 o'clock, I knew I wouldn't be able to get to sleep unless I quieted the howling in my stomach with something, however small. Even then, I fed myself reluctantly, resenting my body's inability to control its needs. For several weeks I lived on bread and butter sprinkled with cinnamon and sugar.

One particularly bad day, when I woke up in the morning and knew that even hearing the phone ring would send me over the edge once and for all, I took myself to a matinee of *Girl, Interrupted.* I was feeling a little crazy myself, and sitting in a theater alone with my anxiety seemed like a good idea. Like being forced to acknowledge the mug on the kitchen table, I think what I really wanted was to stare at the crazy girls on the screen and dare them to ask me what my problem was. Or maybe I was hoping that they, with all their vast experience, would tell me.

As I sat there in the dark, watching the characters peel away the layers of their lives to reveal the causes of their various behaviors, I began to feel a little better. It always helps, when you're feeling not very good about yourself, to look at people who are worse off. At the same time, though, I had a vague suspicion that maybe I wasn't so far away from becoming those girls, especially if anyone was paying close attention. When I left the theater, I made sure no one was following me.

That night, because I couldn't sleep, I turned on the light and read. I picked up *Traveling Mercies,* Anne Lamott's book about faith. Anne and I are pretty much the same person, except that she doesn't have a penis and I'm not an alcoholic. I've always loved her books because I just know she's writing them specifically to me. Except for this latest one, which is all about her attraction to Christianity, a faith that left me cold long ago. Still, Anne is funny and clumsily wise even when I don't get into her particular brand of spirituality, so I kept reading. And almost at the end of the book, when I was so tired I could barely keep my eyes open, I read the following:

> The truth is that your spirits don't rise until you get *way* down. Maybe it's because this—the mud, the bottom—is where it all rises from. Maybe without it, whatever rises would fly off or evaporate before you could even be with it for a moment.

I read this section several times, with a growing resentment. I was angry at Anne for tricking me into realizing what I'd been doing to myself. I hated her for so swiftly and mercilessly ripping off the scab that I'd been picking at piece by piece for the past two months. I was so mad that I almost picked up the phone and called her to tell her what a shit she was.

Instead, I got out of bed and took the dog for a very long walk in the cold, thin light of a winter dawn. We walked for a long time, while the sun came up and I finally let go of the depression I'd gathered around me like extra clothes. I let go of the anxiety about work, and money, and the future. I let myself enjoy, for the first time in weeks, the fact that I can do something wonderful with my writing. And when I came home, I took the mug from the kitchen table, rinsed it out, and made myself some tea. Sitting at my desk, I drank from the mug that no longer symbolized failure to me. And I began to write.

ABOUT THE AUTHOR

Michael Thomas Ford is the author of three previous essay collections: *Alec Baldwin Doesn't Love Me, That's Mr. Faggot to You,* and *It's Not Mean If It's True,* which earned him back-to-back Lambda Literary Awards for humor. He has also recorded an audio book, *My Queer Life,* and written the libretto for *Alec Baldwin Doesn't Love Me,* a musical based on his work. You can visit him at www.michaelthomasford.com.